PREACHING ON YOUR FEET

CONNECTING GOD AND THE AUDIENCE IN THE PREACHABLE MOMENT

FRED R. LYBRAND

ACADEMIC

NASHVILLE, TENNESSEE

Copyright © 2008
by Fred R. Lybrand
All rights reserved.
Printed in the United States of America.

978-0-8054-4686-9

Published by B&H Publishing Group
Nashville, Tennessee

Dewey Decimal Classification: 251
Subject Heading: PREACHING\MINISTRY\PASTORAL
THEOLOGY

1 2 3 4 5 6 7 8 9 10 11 12 • 16 15 14 13 12 11 10 09 08
VP

Contents

Preface

I hope you'll read this preface and not skip it as I do most books. It strikes me that I should tell you, the reader, who exactly I had in mind as I wrote this book. Knowing this audience up front may explain some of my comments, and it also may help you decide if you match the heart of my hope. In my mind I'm thinking about a new preacher who is fresh out of seminary or who has recently received a call to ministry and has in his heart the hope of touching the world through the proclamation of the Word of God. It's a stage of excitement and dreams and ideals—high goals for how explaining the Word of God with passion can catch fire in the souls of those who hear. I'm thinking of that young person or new person in the ministry who sees preaching the Word of God as an awesome responsibility with eternal impact.

The second person in my mind is an older preacher, one who has been at the work long enough to know the realities of study, the realities of audiences, and the realities of what people will learn and won't learn. This second individual is not without hopes and not without interest in the purposes of God; he still labors and is confident that hearing "well done" is well worth the work. This second individual, however, is like someone who is beginning to catch a virus; somewhere in his body he can tell something's wrong, not quite noticeable, unclear exactly what it is; and yet there remains a sense that things are not quite right. He's been to seminars, he's read books, he's tried different things. Even on occasion (perhaps often) he simply purchased and repeated a "proven" sermon from someone else who's usually famous.

In both cases what is at issue is the "more" that is out there. I truly believe that in all the opportunities to blame different things for the state of Christianity, which under the circumstances I'm not convinced is as bad as statisticians claim, I think the heart of the issue for vibrancy or shallowness in Christianity is the pulpit. It has been a special characteristic of Christianity, and historically consistent, that strong pulpits lead to strong churches, weak pulpits to weak churches, and the strength of the churches is the strength of Christianity. Even as I write these words, I think of my childhood church which I visited again not too long ago and remain shocked at a twelve-minute sermon which borrows a thought from a passage and tries to illustrate it briefly before moving on in the liturgy. Now of course I'm confident the preacher is good, but the whole denomination has that orientation. My conviction is simply shame on independent churches and denominational churches that have reduced the preaching of the Word of God to short homilies with limited value and an eye toward entertainment. In Spurgeon's words I believe we need "soul-moving preachers"; and yet to be a soul-moving preacher, mustn't our own souls be moved as preachers?

In these beginning words I also want to explain my qualification for addressing this topic. First, I grew up in the home of an orator. My dad served in the Alabama legislature and received the *Birmingham News* award for outstanding orator of the state senate in the 1970s. I have been speaking publicly for 35 years and have maintained a consistent pulpit ministry for the last 21. I currently preach to around 700 individuals every Sunday morning over three services. I taught speech communication at the University of Alabama for two years and have a library approaching a hundred volumes in homiletics alone.

It is important to understand, however, that I don't think any of these things qualify me to speak on this topic. The only qualification I offer is that about thirteen years ago I came to a crisis point in ministry; I came close to quitting preaching. If it were not for the lessons I will share in this book, I would not be in ministry today. My qualification is that I have begun to learn to preach on my feet, and as I do so, I find preaching a joy and not a burden. I see God in His kindness use the words I share from His Word to touch lives. I see Him give me back time and energy and hope and a constant readiness to open truth to whomever will listen.

I have in mind this young, new, idealistic preacher and this older, concerned but still hopeful, seasoned preacher that both might embrace the principles of preaching on their feet and see a path to soul-moving preaching open before them. I hope these individuals and countless others might become part of a growing movement of well-studied leaders of God who walk well, walk carefully, fill their souls with truth, and pour it out from the pulpit.

It is difficult to measure the impact of certain leaders and their theologies on Christian history, but Karl Barth certainly ranks among the great ones, at least in the last century, carrying on influence to this very day. It may be that something he expressed in preaching the gospel underscores the problem or the challenges we have today, even as we consider the possibility of preaching a message from our hearts to the hearts of those who listen. Read his words:

> There are a number of rules which should be observed in composing a sermon. First, a sermon should be *written*; this is so important that it is necessary to give reasons for it. Certainly the preacher will be giving an address, but whether or not he has the necessary capacity for doing so, he should not simply wait for the Holy Spirit, or any other spirit, to inspire him at the moment of speaking. A sermon must be prepared and drafted word by word. It is certainly true in this instance that an account will have to be given for every idle word. Preaching is not an art in which some are able to improvise while others have to write everything out; it is the central action of evangelical worship in close association with the sacrament. Only a sermon in which every word can be justified may be said to be a sacramental action. The responsibility which attaches to every word he utters is a part of the sanctification of the minister. This rule holds for every preacher and not only for the young. Some ministers have acquired such facility in preaching that they feel able to dispense with this discipline, but their sermons are not Christian discourses.[1]

---

[1] Karl Barth, *The Preaching of the Gospel*, trans. B. E. Hooke (Philadelphia: Westminster, 1963), 77–78.

The influence of this kind of reasoning is difficult to quantify, and yet if a theologian of Barth's stature instructs us never to say a word that was not first written, imagine what happens. If a theologian of Barth's stature tells us never to listen to any spirit in the moment, imagine what is missed in God's work among us. Of course, even to the layman, one can appreciate the fact that there must be a dependence on the Spirit, whether one is crafting words at his desk or sculpting a truth before the eyes of an audience as he pours out his heart for their souls.

The work you have in your hands is a fresh fruit with ancient roots. I think of it as "preaching on your feet," but I'm not alone; in 1947 Gerald Kennedy declared, "'Any man can learn to stand on his feet and preach with freedom.' Any man can master this technique providing he's willing to undergo the necessary self-discipline."[2]

---

[2] John A. Broadus and Vernon L. Stanfield, *On the Preparation and Delivery of Sermons*, 4th ed. (San Francisco: Harper & Row, 1979), 276; quoted sentence is from Gerald Kennedy, *His Word through Preaching* (New York: Harper, 1947), 89.

Chapter 1

Preaching on Your Feet—Its Offer and Our Need

Maximus vero studiourm fructus est, et velut praemium quoddam
amplissimum longi laboris, ex tempore dicendi facultas.
—Quintilian[1]

*A*t the outset it seems that quoting Latin could be the best illustration possible for what "preaching on your feet" is really about. You may not have much experience with Latin, but you may be able to pick out a few words, like *fructus* means fruit or profit, and *laboris* means labor. But quite frankly, most of us would have great difficulty really appreciating what in the world the Latin above is about without knowing that language. We do much the same in our preaching. We speak in a language and communicate to others as though we both entered from different worlds. What has happened

---

[1] Epigraph taken from Henry Ware Jr., *Hints on Extemporaneous Preaching* (Boston: Hilliard, Gray, Little and Wilkins, 1831), epigraph, http://www.prism. net/user/fcarpenter/warejr.html (accessed July 13, 2007).

through the centuries? What makes an excellent preacher distinct from a mediocre one? The claim here is simply that the most effective preachers are those who preach on their feet, and the least effective ones are those who preach on their seats. "Preaching on your seat" is what most schools teach these days and indeed have done so almost exclusively since around 1960. Preaching on your seat is the process of working out copious notes or a manuscript or thick outline in the days ahead of preaching to be practiced and then finally delivered to the audience as a carefully crafted sermon. Excepting those who are excellent actors, preaching on your seat is vastly inferior to preaching on your feet because it misses the most obvious biblical fact regarding preaching: preaching is about connecting a message from God through the preacher to the audience in the moment. Koller sums it up well: "Andrew W. Blackwood reminds us that note free preaching was the method of Jesus and the prophets and apostles who, when they preached, spoke 'from heart to heart and from eye to eye.'"[2]

Preaching on your feet is what preaching has always been—a real connection to real human beings in a real moment in time. In preparation for this book, I was in a conversation with a seminary professor who said, in the midst of the conversation, that I would need to demonstrate my premise biblically, that is, the idea of preaching on your feet. I looked at him and responded, "Let me see if I understand you. I need to demonstrate biblically that no one in the entire Word of God ever used a manuscript or a set of notes when delivering a sermon (Ezra's reading of the Scripture, etc.,

---

[2] Charles W. Koller, *Expository Preaching without Notes,* in *How to Preach without Notes* (Grand Rapids: Baker, 1964), 1:35, quoting Andrew W. Blackwood, *The Preparation of Sermons* (New York: Abingdon, 1948), 27.

hardly qualifies)?" He smiled, I smiled, and we continued with lunch. The reality is that just as Blackwood observes, Jesus spoke from "heart to heart and from eye to eye." Preaching on your feet offers, by the very design of God, the means through which we can speak "heart to heart and eye to eye" to the people we serve.

Now back to the Latin; roughly translated, this quote from Quintilian comes out as follows:

> But the richest fruit of all our study, and the most ample recompense for the extent of our labor, is the faculty of speaking extempore.[3]

Thus far we have seen words used like "free delivery" and "extemporaneous" rather than a statement about preaching on your feet, and yet historically this is exactly the understanding of what "preaching on your feet" was all about. It is the fruit of long labor, and it is a skill that comes easier with age. It is also, however, a special kind of skill that engages all that a person has to persuade an audience of all that God offers. Imagine how your steady work, day in and day out, in wrestling with God, in thinking theologically, in abiding in Christ, in praying before the Lord, in wrestling in discussions, in teaching Bible studies, in pondering moments in nature or in traffic when God offers an illustration just right for a particular truth. Imagine all these things coming together in a moment, and after reflection and preparation you are standing before the congregation and pouring out in a clear, passionate style your heartbeat concerning a truth that is needed by the hearts of those who listen. This is what

---

[3] James M. Buckley, *Extemporaneous Oratory for Professional and Amateur Speakers* (New York: Eaton & Mains, 1898), 344–45.

preaching on your feet offers, in its worse moments, to both you and your audience.

Echo

Consider for a moment a strategic word for understanding the value of preaching on your feet. It is the word *echo*. Phillips Brooks, in his *Lectures on Preaching*, instructs the students in his lectures at Yale Divinity School in the 1800s with the following:

> I want to make you know two things: first, that if your ministry is to be good for anything, it must be your ministry, and not a feeble echo of another man's; and, second, that the Christian ministry is not the mere practice of a set of rules and precedents, but is a broad, free, fresh meeting of a man with men, in such close contact that the Christ who has entered into his life may, through his, enter into theirs.[4]

Brooks gives us the word *echo*. An echo is a proper way to think about mimicked, indirect, or distant ministry. That echo, as we all know, is the essential reflection of sound—that is, a copy of the original.

When a preacher of the Word of God preaches another's sermon or attempts to sound like another famed preacher, he is engaged in the process of being an echo rather than an original voice. Even when one reads aloud his own writing, it still has the flavor of echo. When one works at his desk and labors to write a manuscript, when one works at his desk

---

[4] Phillips Brooks, *The Joy of Preaching* (Grand Rapids: Kregel, 1989), 88, originally published as *Lectures on Preaching*, 1877.

4

and labors to write an outline, he is in that moment guessing about his audience because he does not know exactly what will transpire between that moment at his desk and the lives of the people. He cannot exactly know the configuration of who's in attendance and who's missing. He further cannot know what experiences and reflection and insight will occur between the completion of the sermon and the moment before the people.

Years ago I had a conversation with the elders of the church I was then serving, explaining my discoveries and burden to learn to preach on my feet. In that discussion I observed to them that between the time I finish a sermon on a Thursday or Friday and the delivery of the sermon on Sunday, I continue to grow in the Lord; therefore, if I preached on Sunday something I concluded on a Friday, it's plagiarism because it was written by another person (that is, who I was on Friday)! You may think this is a play on logic, but it's actually a play on truth. We are the person we are in the moment we preach; and when we copy, even ourselves, it has the cavernous sound of an echo.

It is my understanding that one of the most famous Christian leaders in our day encourages people to purchase his transcripts and preach his sermons. It is rumored that somewhere near 80,000 preachers every Sunday do that very thing. There are other preaching services where transcripts are available and sermons may be preached. Sometimes the use of another's sermons is a known fact; sometimes it's plagiarized, passed off as if it were one's own thoughts. In either event these things are echoes.

The echo itself can be even more graphically appreciated by picking up a sermon of Charles Haddon Spurgeon.

Spurgeon is one of the most famous preachers in history and largely was a preach-on-your-feet man. If you were to pick up one of Spurgeon's sermons and simply read it to your congregation, albeit with passion and energy, it would still carry the problem of echo. Let me offer an example. In a sermon entitled "How Saints May Help the Devil," his opening words are as follows:

> It is not a comfortable state to be at enmity with God, and the sinner knows this. Although he perseveres in his rebellion against the Most High, and turns not at the rebuke of the Almighty, but still goeth on in his iniquity, desperately seeking his own destruction, yet is he aware in his own conscience that he is not in a secure position.[5]

If Spurgeon were here today and he spoke like this, he would not be famous; he would be strange. But Spurgeon, if he were here today, would not speak in that language; he would speak in the language of the common man. Hear Spurgeon's own words: "Let your oratory, therefore, constantly improve in clearness, cogency, naturalness, and persuasiveness. Try, dear brethren, to get such a style of speaking that you *suit yourselves to your audiences*. Much lies in that."[6]

To pick up Spurgeon and read him to your congregation would be an act of trying to pass off an echo that is even more distant due to time. James Buckley offers this observation: "When looking away from the paper and repeating

---

[5] Charles Haddon Spurgeon, "How Saints May Help the Devil," in *Spurgeon's Sermons* (1883; repr., Grand Rapids: Baker, n.d.), 6:125.

[6] C. H. Spurgeon, *Lectures to My Students, Complete and Unabridged* (Grand Rapids: Zondervan, 1954), 211.

a sentence, his face cannot light up as does he who speaks directly to the people."[7] Preaching on your feet is about speaking directly to the people and not through an echo.

Our Need

What do we need in preaching? What, in particular as an audience, what in particular as Christians in America, do we need from the pulpit and from the preacher? Joseph Webb, in his volume *Preaching without Notes*, makes two observations concerning a "national statement" based on 400 hours of conversation with 700 Methodist laity and clergy in 13 regional events. After listing the study's conclusions, which included statements such as, "There's widespread disappointment that so much preaching lacks enthusiasm for the gospel," he states:

> Two things in particular arise from this statement, however; one overtly, the other somewhat covertly. The first is that preachers who play down the importance of preaching are out of sync with what their congregations want most, which is the highest quality preaching possible. The second thing in the statement, however, appears in the last sentence. It is that laypeople tend to believe that preachers, by and large, are not doing the best possible job that they could do in the pulpit, and that their chief failing is not theological or pastoral; it is a failure in public speaking.[8]

---

[7] Buckley, *Extemporaneous Oratory*, 14.
[8] Joseph M. Webb, *Preaching without Notes* (Nashville: Abingdon, 2001), 24–25.

At the core it is a failure in public speaking. What hope do we have for developing excellent preachers if we're engaged in a process of writing as though it were public speaking? And what hope do we have of developing preachers if the growing masses of preachers defer to sharing an echo by weekly reading the sermon of another preacher?

It strikes me that the glaring metaphor is meal preparation. Are we offering packages from a vending machine as a meal? A vending machine offers something we might call "food," and it truly might have some nutrition to it, but by and large vending machine food will kill people who live on it alone. The second analogy is the TV dinner, which comes to us by mass production and is somewhat nutritional in a heat-and-serve fashion. The final example is a chef who has learned to create nutritious meals for the moment; this is what preaching is intended to be, and a real meal by a real chef is exactly what is needed by the congregations of today or of any era.

In the simplest of terms, what we need most in our preaching is life, relevance, and connection. We need *life* in our preaching, as Brooks said, a connection of man to men, of person to person—someone who is abiding, someone who is alive with the truth, someone who owns and possesses from long labor and a walk with God, life for lives. Second, our preaching should be *relevant*. Our messages should take eternal, transcultural principles and bring them to bear in a relevant way to the lives of those who listen. It is not simply connecting the dots in the understanding of the audience, but it is connecting the dots of truth with the lives they live. Jesus Christ Himself was a master on this point. He spoke to the people according to their needs and according to terms they understood: bread of life, vine and branches, fishermen, sheep, coins; and the list goes on. Finally, our preaching needs to *connect*. This is more than a clever sales notion; it is actually a transaction of spirit-to-spirit communication. It is an authentic connection as a person who lives among people, understands their lives beyond his own life, beyond relevance in the message, and authentically stands on his feet and connects directly to the people.

A written or outlined sermon could, quite frankly, be done by anyone and probably done better by someone else skilled in the art of acting. Webb offers a little insight on why preaching on our feet helps us connect to people. He says:

> Congregants, too, are smart people. They appreciate and learn from straight-forward explanation of things, even theological things. They do not worry about the preacher tripping over a word or a phrase; they understand how we all talk. They also want to learn theology and doctrine. So the word comes unspoken to the preacher from the congregants: "Tell us about your faith, and ours. Tell us about theology, what it is and how it works. Tell us what you have learned about it and how you have come to think about it and internalize it yourself. Share with us the issues of theology and how that theology impinges on us. Share stories with us. Give us reason to laugh. But talk to us about the hard stuff as well. Don't read it to us. Talk to us."[9]

---

[9] Ibid., 32–33.

Webb is right, and any student of communication understands it. Human beings are interested in real live communication. They're not concerned about tripping over a word or phrase. In fact, that aspect of being a human being tends to endear congregants. Only the professors and the grammarians in our culture are concerned about everything being said just right. People want a real person to tell them the truth. Preaching on your feet uniquely and naturally meets these needs.

At no time has our culture been more ripe with the need for preachers to recover and grow in this historically proven approach to communicating truth. Roy H. Williams, the founder of Wizard Academy, a marketing and training company, made the following observation, which is about the best advice a preacher could get as well, in the following e-letter:

Blogs and Reality TV: The Changing Face of America

Do you remember when America watched awards shows?

If you were somehow unplugged and didn't receive the newsflash, the combined strength of Paul McCartney, Madonna, U2, Mariah Carey, Coldplay, Faith Hill, and Jay-Z wasn't enough to swing the hammer and ring the bell during this year's Grammy Awards. A frail 17 million watched these legends read their cue cards while a muscular 28.3 million cheered hopeful, nameless kids singing their hearts out on American Idol.

It was just one more indication of how we're moving away from the vertical hero worship of idealism to establish the horizontal links that mark an emerging civic generation.

Grandpa Jagger during halftime at the Super Bowl, surrounded by people doing their best to act like cheering fans . . . I'm sorry, but that was just sad.

I'm not trying to be catty; I'm trying to make a point: Plastic posing bores us. We have no desire to hear another Miss America contestant talk about her dream of world peace. Just once, wouldn't you like to hear the interviewer say, "And how is walking around in high heels and a swimsuit going to help bring about world peace?"

Unfiltered authenticity is the new cool. And volunteerism is on the rise.

We don't listen to big talkers anymore. Our collective silence toward them is our way of saying, "Talk is cheap. Do something."

Tom Hanks is the new John Wayne. Remember Hanks' portrayal of the dutiful but reluctant English-teacher-turned-soldier in *Saving Private Ryan*? He was just a regular guy, doing the best he could, trying to make the best of a bad situation. Kind of like you and me.

Struggling, flawed, tormented Jason Bourne is the new James Bond.

Lost in Translation is the new *Love Story*.

I'm not trying to depress you. I'm just trying to open your eyes to the realities of the new marketplace.

Hype is dead.

11

In 2004—the first year following the shift away from idealism—the Grammys scored a respectable 26.3 million viewers. The next year they fell to just 18.8 million. So this year's 17 million should have come as no surprise.

Anyone taking bets on next year's audience?

If you're a business owner needing advice about marketing in the new millennia, here's all you really need to know:

Say it straight. Say it real. You'll do fine.[10]

How would your ministry change if you could rise at a moment's notice and give a commendable sermon straight from God's Word and your heart? So what's stopping you? Perhaps it's about pain and pleasure.

Preaching is joy, but preparing is torture. Maybe this doesn't ring true for you; maybe you're one who finds the preaching the pain, while the preparation is the pleasure. Personally, I wasn't fond of either until I discovered what preaching was really about. I'm not writing for preachers alone but for preachers especially. We've lost something in America; we've lost something in our pulpits; we've lost the skill of authentic heart-to-heart communication. Of course not everyone is at a loss. Some preachers capture audiences and impact the masses, but it isn't common; it isn't even normal. What has happened? What needs to happen? Explaining what has happened may be beyond our ability to know, but we can speculate. Some would say our content has softened. Others would argue that we are not empowered by the Spirit.

---

[10] Roy H. Williams, "Blogs and Reality TV: The Changing Face of America," *Monday Morning Memo*, Wizard Academy, February 20 2006, http://www.wizardacademy.com/showmemo.asp?id=289 (accessed February 20, 2006).

Others still say we need more prayer or teachable people or illustrations in abundance.

I want to offer a different paradigm: I think our problem is that we lack preachers. We lack individuals who open God's Word to others through their own unique style and experiences. Seminaries are in part to blame. In seminary, students pay money and work hard to learn doctrine and skills. During this period, and understandably so, students become enamored with professors and try to emulate them. Though trying to be like someone is understandable, it won't lead to authentic preaching. Why? First, because it squelches the uniqueness of the preacher's personality. Second, the preacher follows the examples, not of preachers but of professors. Unless the local church is a classroom, the last thing it needs is the intensity afforded a Greek class. The pulpit is for people, common people, who, though bright, are busy trying to sort out life in the daily world. Is it any wonder that the Natural Church Development[11] researchers have found "pastor as theologian" to be a negative correlation with church health and growth? Specifically they have found that often the more education a pastor has the less health the church enjoys.

Hype is dead, but it was never alive to begin with. We need preachers of the Word of God who shine through with an unquenchable authenticity; fresh voices, alive, burdened, and authoritatively original. We need true preachers who can "preach on their feet."

---

[11] Christian A. Schwartz, *Natural Church Development: A Guide to Eight Essential Qualities of Healthy Churches* (Carol Stream, IL: ChurchSmart Resources, 1996).

Chapter 2

Preaching on Your
Feet Defined

J think about definitions all the time. I don't like
to eat a dish that isn't properly named, and I
don't like the word *surprise* in a cuisine's title.
(One comedian observed that pig snout is usually the key
ingredient when the word *surprise* is used.) I like definitions
for a couple of reasons. First, I like to communicate well, and
I've found definitions are vital for effective communication.

Among my most challenging experiences in communication occurred during my seminary days when our good friend
Melody Elefson and I went back and forth about a Southern
delicacy. I hale from Alabama while Melody grew up in the
Northwest. I innocently asked her one day, "Melody, have
you ever had boiled peanuts?" In the South fresh peanuts are
boiled in a salty brine soup, drained, and sold in a plastic bag
with a name like "Joe's Eats" stamped on the label. Boiled
peanuts work much like potato chips; you eat one, get an
overdose of salt, then eat the whole bag trying to reexperi-
ence the first jolt. Melody responded with neither a yes nor

a no. Instead she simply asked me, "Bold Peanuts?" "No," I said, "Boiled peanuts." She said, "Bold?" I said "boiled" . . . until it began to smell like the Mason-Dixon Line was getting drawn again. In a moment of God's mercy, I realized it must sound like I was saying, "Bulled peanuts." Quickly I exaggerated the vowels and said, "Boy-ill-duh peanuts." She smiled with recognition and declared, "No!" It wasn't just pronunciation because Melody had no idea, no definition, which included such bizarre mistreatment of a peanut. Definitions are essential to communication.

The second reason I love definitions is that I loathe conflict. A little quote from Nathaniel Emmons I stumbled upon has served me often in overcoming conflict: "Just definitions either prevent or put an end to disputes."[1] Most battles people create are born from a conflict between opinion and fact. Facts tend to be indisputable; hence no disputes occur around them. On the other hand, "facts in dispute" turn out to be opinions rather than settled bits of information. Only days ago three of our children dragged their mother into a debate about the size of a sloth, a tree-hanging animal. It turns out some of the kids were hot because Mom said sloths are "big" while others insisted they are small. I showed up in the middle of this important question and announced, "Hey, we can look it up and know for sure!" Miraculously everyone stopped the discussion (I don't think they've checked it out yet either).

The Search for the Right Word

Defining preaching on your feet demands a search for the right word. I have found few books written since about

---

[1] http://www.quotationspage.com/quote/29057.html (accessed July 13, 2007).

1960 that fully address this subject. Through the years, in fact through the ages, a host of preachers and authors have touted the value, power, and usefulness of preaching on your feet; but they use terms to describe this approach to preaching that really won't work today. The phrase "won't work" is probably not right; it would however take a significant amount of reeducation even to have a conversation regarding the subject. In the writings of insightful preachers of time past, words like *extemporaneous* and *impromptu* appear again and again. "Free delivery," "platform speaking," and "open-air preaching" all carry the same basic idea. These terms, however, have come to suggest unpreparedness, talking off the top of one's head, rising just to say anything— which, of course, reduces Christian preaching to little more than spouting opinion without any labor, reflection, or hard work. The history of preaching on your feet, the history of extemporaneous preaching, the history of good impromptu discussion, is also the history of the Western world in areas such as oration and Socratic method. Spurgeon, we'll see, talks of this art form, this skill, this ability as that of a "practiced thinker"—that phrase itself leads us in the right direction while we're searching for the right word or words.

There's another issue related to this search for the right word: the concept itself has become so marred in the minds of so many that any definition that isn't pronounced just right or means just the right thing is subject to instant disregard. The training I received in seminary, and indeed much of the training continued to this day, suggests that preaching on your feet is not profitable, prudent, or practical for any proclaimer of the truth of God.

Recently two students were overheard discussing with great energy the "fact" that preaching without manuscripting your sermon will lead to heresy. You see, in the minds of scholars (those who teach pastors how to serve in local churches?) the most critical thing is to be careful in wording and phrasing. Indeed, it is the responsibility of scholars to be careful, precise, and articulate. Pastors have the same responsibility to be careful, to be articulate, to be as precise as possible; however, the exactitude of scholarship and the ridicule fellow scholars will give one another in print is not the same minefield for the preacher. The preacher is interacting with largely untrained individuals who are interested in understanding the simplicity and purity of devotion to Christ. It means nothing to an audience for a preacher to slip up on a word or two, when his heart and his thoughts are reaching to their need with a message from God. That different world, the world in which the preacher ministers, invites a different form of communication, a form of communication we'll call preaching on our feet.

What We Do Not Mean by Preaching on Our Feet

Definitions, as we learn, require some sense of what is not meant by a particular term in order to create a clear contrast for understanding. Charles Haddon Spurgeon, famed for his study, his prolific publications, and his enduring impact among the most widely published Christians in history, made this observation:

> Unstudied thoughts coming from the mind
> without previous research, without the subjects in

hand having been investigated at all, must be of a
very inferior quality, even from the most superior
men; and as none of us would have the effrontery
to glorify ourselves as men of genius or wonders of
erudition, I fear that our unpremeditated thoughts
upon most subjects would not be remarkably worthy of attention.[2]

Spurgeon is speaking of the faculty of impromptu speech
and at times in his essay seems to contradict himself because
he actually is emphasizing the importance of this extemporaneous ability to reflect and communicate as a practiced
thinker. He is warning against "unpremeditated thoughts,"
that is, things that have not been pondered, truths in the
Word of God that have only superficially been considered.
These are not what we mean by preaching on your feet. We
do not mean to rise and speak with some vague notion, or no
notion at all, and pontificate under the assumed direction of
the Holy Spirit as a performer before his audience. Spurgeon
goes on to say about impromptu speech: "Good impromptu
speech is just the utterance of a practiced thinker—a man
of information, meditating on his legs, and allowing his
thoughts to march through his mouth into the open air. Think
aloud as much as you can when you're alone, and you will
soon be on the high road to success in this matter."[3] So, however Spurgeon thought of this faculty of impromptu speech
in the negative, he also saw great value in this ability to be
a "practiced thinker." Spurgeon most assuredly meant well-
considered and well-studied communication.

---

[2] C. H. Spurgeon, *Lectures to My Students, Complete and Unabridged* (Grand
Rapids: Zondervan, 1954), 140.
[3] Ibid., 149.

In clarifying what he does not mean, however, he also adds this to the conversation: "We do not recommend the plan of learning sermons by heart, and repeating them from memory; that is both a wearisome exercise of an inferior power of mind and an indolent neglect of other and superior faculties."[4] Here Spurgeon is clarifying what we do not mean by preaching on your feet. We do not mean working out a full plan and memorizing it, committing to using the faculty of the memory to store a well-prepared message much as we might memorize a poem or a quote, or sometimes even a joke.

In a similar way, some authors have presented a near cousin to preaching on your feet: preaching without notes. Joseph M. Webb, for example, in his book by the same title, makes preaching without notes an act of having the sermon in your head but not carrying notes with you into the pulpit. For example he says:

> The point here is that despite the details that must be learned, it works. I know the whole thing fairly well after the first hour, I repeat the process in exactly the same way during the second hour the next day, by the end of the second hour, I know the sermon's outline, including all of its details, by heart. On Saturday, I will go through it again a few times, but only to sharpen it up. After a refresher early Sunday I am ready to preach the sermon.[5]

---

[4] Ibid., 142.
[5] Joseph M. Webb, *Preaching without Notes* (Nashville: Abingdon, 2001), 95.

This turns out to be something other than preaching on your feet. It doesn't have the advantages, the insight, and the freshness that come through what we will offer in this book. Webb adds: "While it is clearly the task of the preacher without notes to stay close to the well-prepared and memorized outline, one will discover very quickly that there are clearly times when unexpected insights occur to one while one is actually preaching."[6] "Actually preaching" is a striking phrase, for if preaching on your feet is about anything, it is indeed about actually preaching. Webb is instructing the preacher not to take notes into the pulpit but to have the notes cleanly in his head. Preaching on your feet is not about memorizing an outline or having a full set of notes in your head. Those devices are simply illusions to make it appear to the audience that you are note free. If, however, your notes are memorized, or if your notes are before you on paper, you're still using notes instead of "actually preaching."

What We Do Mean by Preaching on Your Feet

Preaching on your feet is a relationship between hearts. In preaching there is the heart of God, the heart of the preacher, and hearts in the audience. These hearts are to be connected authentically in a fresh and living way. Preaching on your feet is about the very activity on the part of the preacher which brings these people together. It goes without saying that a preacher is to walk with God, a preacher is to pray, and a preacher is to know his sheep; however, the act of preaching in the proper sense of the word involves a relationship between this walk with God, study and reflection, a strategy concerning the truth at hand, and a connection with the audi-

---

[6] Ibid., 115.

ence in words from the heart. Phillips Brooks put it in these simple words:

> The real question about a sermon is, not whether it is extemporaneous when you deliver it to your people, but whether it ever was extemporaneous, whether there was ever a time when the discourse sprang freshly from your heart and mind. The main difference in sermons is that some sermons are, and some sermons are not, conscious of an audience. The main question about sermons is whether they feel their hearers.[7]

Spurgeon ends his famous essay on the faculty of impromptu speech with these words:

> I might have said much more if I had extended the subject to what is *usually called* extempore preaching, that is to say, the preparation of the sermon so far as thoughts go, and leaving the words to be found during delivery; but this is quite another matter, and although looked upon as a great attainment by some, it is, as I believe, an indispensable requisite for the pulpit, and by no means a mere luxury of talent; but of this we will speak on another occasion.[8]

Spurgeon helps us here by stressing the fact that hard work and study precede the act of preaching. This is not simply the talent of a practiced thinker but a skill developed along, one

---

[7] Phillips Brooks, *The Joy of Preaching* (Grand Rapids: Kregel, 1989), 130, originally published as *Lectures on Preaching*, 1877.
[8] Spurgeon, *Lectures to My Students*, 153.

hopes, with a gift which involves intense study and an intense heart in pouring out the fruit of study to a needy audience.

The best book on "preaching on your feet" was published in 1898 by James M. Buckley, who offers the clearest definition of what is meant historically by "extemporaneous oratory," or what I believe is best described in our day as preaching on your feet: "The delivery, in an arrangement of words, sentences, and paragraphs, entirely the birth of the occasion, of ideas previously conceived and adopted with more or less fullness and precision, together with such thoughts and feelings as may arise and obtain utterance."[9] Buckley obviously includes both preparation and delivery in his definition but understands that preaching on your feet is about a message delivered in the moment to an audience who is there for the purpose of receiving the message. This contrasts with preparation that culminates in a written manuscript or a very thick outline. In the instance of a manuscript or notes, the design of the message is largely unrelated to the audience (since the audience is only imagined and not real) and largely unrelated to the moment in time since it is prepared completely beforehand. Delivery for the thick outline or the written manuscript turns into a performance rather than a true connection or communication with the listeners.

For Buckley, preaching is "entirely the birth of the occasion"; this brings the idea of preaching on your feet to the event of the sermon itself. Preaching is the moment of the sermon that includes the audience, one's walk with God, one's preparation, and things that come to the forefront in the moment to weave together into a unique tapestry of a sermon for people in a time. Notice also that Buckley refers to

---

[9] Buckley, *Extemporaneous Oratory*, 10.

preparation when he speaks of "ideas previously conceived." He tells his reader that he is not speaking of making something up in the moment but rather of reflection, study, preparation—all involved in the process leading up to the moment of delivery. Preaching on your feet also by its nature includes Buckley's point regarding precision since when we speak in a moment, our precision is necessarily lessened compared to the tedious nature of revising a written work. In this regard much of our preaching has been sifted and refined and carefully constructed such that it is not only precise; it is often sterile. Buckley's definition leaves room for insight, spontaneous leading of the Spirit, grace, connection, a reaching to the audience in a moment with a sermon intended and given just for them. He also includes the fact that feelings can be included in this process, "such thoughts and feelings as may arise and obtain utterance." In manuscript form only thoughts can be captured. In a thick outline only thoughts can be organized. Feelings that arise in the act of preaching when there's no room in the sermon for them to be expressed are simply fought against and avoided although they are often the most powerful piece because human beings hear another human being speak from his heart.

Buckley gives us further insight for our definition of preaching on your feet by describing what is going on inside the preacher as he preaches. It isn't enough to say, "Don't use a manuscript, and don't use a thick outline; study well, then deliver in the moment." What is preaching on your feet like from inside the preacher? As you perhaps find the courage or faith or experimental gusto to attempt to learn to preach on your feet, what will go on inside of you? Buckley offers us this insight: "To the consciousness of the speaker his own mental state is similar to that of one participating in an animated conversation—there being no effort to recollect, no anticipation of what is to come, but entire absorption in the process of evolving, in correct forms of speech, the thoughts intended to be impressed."[10]

From my own experience in learning to preach on my feet over the past decade, Buckley's definition from 1898 holds true. In my better moments in preaching on my feet, my mental state is similar to an animated conversation with an audience. I am not trying to recall information. I am not trying to anticipate my points. The nervousness that attends such activity is gone, and I am consumed with the message and the text and what God has for these people before me—these people who are to be loved and fed, challenged and encouraged with the Word of God. Buckley adds, in the same discussion about definition, a nice picture for the preacher engaged in this high form of communication: "If words, phrases, or sentences which have been previously thought are uttered, they are fresh products of thinking, coming without recollection and without summons of the will. They are not brought forth as crystals from a cabinet, but rise as streams from an overflowing fountain."[11]

That is the most powerful picture. We're speaking of life—not a collection of thoughts to bring out of a cabinet to show admiring guests but a flood of thought and feeling and spirit that burst forth to water a dry and parched land.

---

[10] Ibid., 10.
[11] Ibid.

Chapter 3

Three Essentials of Effective Preaching

he object, or objective, of our preaching makes all the difference in the world. Moreover, the object itself calls for different modes of communication. Depending on your objective, your mode of preparation and delivery is largely dictated to you, assuming you want the best possible means to reach your objective. Let me offer an example from attending a variety of scholarly events throughout my tenure in the ministry. When scholars present papers, their objective is precision and clarity, especially as they're introducing a new slant on an old topic. In order to reach their objective of being precise and clear, scholars must speak from a written transcript. Their message is largely deductive (major point, subpoints), and every word has been carefully combed so that all objections and critiques are anticipated in advance. Of course, most of us are bored out of our minds unless the topic is unusually interesting or the speaker deviates from his notes. Indeed, it is a curious thing to watch a speaker read his transcript with all those in the audience reading along; but if he suddenly offers an aside, away from the transcript, you can literally feel the energy in the room change, and the attention of the audience and the connection with the speaker transformed in that momentary stray away from notes.

Charles G. Finney is indeed one of the most famous preachers in American history. You may not particularly like his theology, but the fact that he reached hundreds of thousands of people in his preaching career is almost without parallel in history. He, in his autobiography, replied to critics of his method of preaching:

> In reply to their objections, I have sometimes told them what a judge of the supreme court remarked to me, upon this subject. "Ministers," said he, "do not exercise good sense in addressing the people. They are afraid of repetition. They use language not well understood by the common people. Their illustrations are not taken from the common pursuits of life. They write in too elevated a style, and read without repetition, and are not understood by the people. . . . [Lawyers'] object," he said, "in addressing a jury, is to get their minds settled before they leave the jury box; not to make a speech in language but partially understood by them; not to let ourselves out in illustrations entirely above their apprehension; not to display our oratory, and then let them go. We are set on getting a verdict."[1]

---

[1] Charles G. Finney, *Memoir of Rev. Charles G. Finney: Written by Himself* (New York: Revell, 1876), 85–86.

Finney's point through this judge of the Supreme Court is that preachers are to have an object in view. In parallel with a lawyer, the preacher's purpose is to get a verdict that day with that sermon. Finney goes on to quote the judge:

> "[Ministers] go into their study and write a sermon; they go in their pulpit and read it, and those that listen to it but poorly understand it. Many words used they will not understand, until they go home and consult their dictionaries. They do not address the people, expecting to convince them, and to get their verdict in favor of Christ, upon the spot. They seek no such object."[2]

Preaching is actually about winning the listener to think, feel, and act in accordance with the biblical truth at hand. Sometimes that object is faith in Christ, but at other times it may be letting go of a root of bitterness that has held one captive for decades. The Word of God is the Word from God, and the object, simply put, is to offer the truth in such a way that it changes the whole person.

As this is the object of preaching, three words capture the essential elements necessary for effective preaching. These elements also display why preaching on your feet is the proper mode. Let's consider each of these.

Preaching Essential 1: Persuasion

At its heart, preaching is about persuasion. It is about individuals becoming convinced that a particular truth is not only valid but also important and demanding action before

---

[2] Ibid., 86.

the sunset. A number of Greek words are used in relationship to preaching. *Kerusso*[3] carries the flavor of proclamation, and yet it's an authoritative proclamation that expects the hearer to respond and obey. Another word, more to the heart of the issue, is *peitho*,[4] which means to persuade, particularly to move or affect by kind words or motives. Specifically, it means "to persuade another to receive a belief, meaning to convince somebody, a person or persons" (Acts 14:19; Acts 18:4, "He . . . persuaded . . . both Jews and Greeks," meaning he sought to convince them; 2 Cor 5:11).[5] These passages clarify the point. Each of these passages display that Paul's aim was to persuade them.

This persuasion is not intended to be manipulative or to use some clever sales gimmick but rather to appeal, to issue an invitation to people to let go of their disbeliefs and to embrace the truth. Persuasion can also obviously be directed at an error or falsehood as the crowd was persuaded to stone Paul. The telling nature of Paul's aim in persuasion is found in Acts 26:28: "Then Agrippa said to Paul, 'You almost persuade me to become a Christian.'" The great summary of Paul's focus concerning persuasion and preaching is found in Acts 28:23: "So when they had appointed him a day, many came to him at his lodging, to whom he explained and solemnly testified of the kingdom of God, persuading them concerning Jesus from both the Law of Moses and the Prophets, from morning till evening." It is common knowledge that teachers, by and large, simply lay out a truth and leave it to the individual to sort out what he does with it. The preacher,

[3] W. E. Vine, *Expository Dictionary of Old and New Testament Words* (CD-ROM, Logos Research Systems, 1997).

[4] Ibid.

[5] A. T. Robinson, *Word Pictures in the New Testament* (CD-ROM, Logos Research Systems, 1997).

as designed by God, has a different focus; he is burdened to *persuade*. He is not satisfied with the niceties of affection from an audience that appreciates the value of the truths explained. Instead, the preacher wants the truth embraced and aims to that point, inviting and pleading and clarifying the importance of the truth for that moment, for that audience, for an impact eternally.

Preaching Essential 2: Earnestness

In trying to find the right word to describe this persuasion, terms such as *passion*, *zeal*, and *energy* come to mind. Historically, however, another word has been commonly used, and it is the word *earnestness*. It is common knowledge that classical persuasion involves the Greek notions of ethos, logos, and pathos. Ethos is the ethic or the credibility of the speaker. Logos is the logic or the reasoning along with the evidence. Pathos is the connection, empathetically with the audience. In classical thinking these three elements generated the greatest means of convincing or persuading others. Who can argue with classical thinkers? And yet curiously there is perhaps a hierarchy in these three elements. Education tends to make us think that logic is the telling theme. No doubt, logic and reasoning are priorities to some individuals; furthermore, logic and reasoning have an enduring nature once a person is convinced with evidence and rationale. Unfortunately, the great masses, as any of us can observe, are not particularly won by logic. The character of the individual, too, is certainly important. This ethos is important; however most people do not know much about the speakers they hear on television or radio or perhaps the first time or first several times visiting a church. They make assumptions, and indeed, when a speaker is proven not to have good ethics or character, it turns out to be a deal killer for his persuasiveness until that character issue is resolved, rectified, or forgotten over time.

Pathos: passion, empathy, feeling—this is somehow the thing that persuades. For some reason a passionate, burdened, earnest individual captivates an audience and often persuades individuals to new actions and new convictions due to the passion. As I've reflected on this fact, it strikes me that perhaps this pathos actually ties nicely to the other two elements. An earnest individual is believable as to character because he communicates that he himself is convinced. There is a disconnect when a speaker talks about something important but talks with no passion at all. It affects the perception of his character or his ethics. Passion, or earnestness, also carries within it the labor of logic because of the intimate connection between feelings and thinking. It is not only difficult but also demonstrably impossible for a person to care passionately and be earnest about a point without there being an undercurrent of reasoning and logic that sustains and supports the passion. The logic may not be suitable or formed in perfect syllogisms, according to the evaluation of some, yet there is still a line of reasoning that in combination with the earnestness and what it displays as to the character of the person that comes together and persuades the audience. How sad that we can see this in advertising and public speaking and politics, and yet we as preachers too often have missed this power.

Consider how important earnestness was to some of the great preachers in history. Charles Haddon Spurgeon in *Lectures to My Students* wrote an entire chapter entitled, "Earnestness: Its Marring and Maintenance." Arnold Dallimore, one of Spurgeon's biographers, underscores his earnestness as a theme: "Above all, in his delivery Spurgeon was entirely natural. There was nothing 'put on' about him, and although a note of humor often crept in to what he was saying, the whole of his preaching was overshadowed by his tremendous earnestness."[6] Dallimore adds:

> In seeking to reach these people—indeed, in every aspect of his ministry—Spurgeon was characterized by an earnestness that almost defies description.
>
> Some authors have assumed that he was little more than an entertainer. They picture him as a man who entered the pulpit in a jovial manner, made people laugh and feel good, and who regarded preaching as something of a casual pastime. Nothing can be further from the truth.[7]

Dallimore proves that this kind of earnestness will bring criticism and shows that Spurgeon was more than an entertainer. One of Spurgeon's many critics dismissed him with this caricature:

> His style is that of the vulgar colloquial, varied by rant. . . . All the most solemn mysteries of our holy religion are by him rudely, roughly and impiously handled. Mystery is vulgarized, sanctity profaned, common sense outraged and decency disgusted. . . . His rantings are interspersed with

---

[6] Arnold Dallimore, *Spurgeon* (Chicago: Moody, 1984), 64.
[7] Ibid., 76.

coarse anecdotes that split the ears of groundlings; and this is popularity! this is the "religious furor" of London.[8]

Sadly, we hear similar critiques of popular radio or television preachers in our day. Such a preacher, in Wesley's words, "put himself on fire and people came to watch him burn."[9] These preachers have passion, though some may lack valuable content. Perhaps they are actors, but perhaps they are sincere. Imagine what might happen if well-studied, well-prepared preachers of the Word of God were able to release truth with that passion.

Dallimore finally underscores this earnestness as governing all that Spurgeon was associated with:

> Spurgeon spoke out against the kind of minister who before preaching can be a jolly fellow, happily greeting the people, and who after the service can gather jovially with them at the door, having fair words for all. His place at such time, he declared, is with God, weeping out the failure of his preaching and pleading that the seed sown in hearts might take root and bring forth fruit unto eternal life.
>
> This earnestness characterized the whole service—the singing, the Scripture reading, and the preaching—but it was especially evident as Spurgeon led the congregation in prayer.

[8] Ibid., 65. Dallimore found this in Iain Murray, ed., *The Early Years* (London: Banner of Truth, 1962), 311, who took this from a critique found originally in the *Essex Standard*.

[9] "Sleepy Preachers," A.M.G. Bible Illustration Series (Chattanooga, TN: A.M.G. Publishers, 2000), [CD-ROM] (Oak Harbor, WA.: Logos Research Systems, Inc., 1997).

Throughout his entire ministry many hearers remarked that, moved as they were by his preaching, they were still more affected by his praying. D. L. Moody, after his first visit to England, being asked upon his return to America, "Did you hear Spurgeon preach?" replied, "Yes, but better still, I heard him pray."[10]

It is common for the people to notice and appreciate when their pastor prays because there are no notes, and especially when he prays according to a burden on his heart, earnestness appears.

In Spurgeon's own words the importance of earnestness is explained in his *Lectures to My Students*:

Now, in order that we may be acceptable, *we must be earnest when actually engaged in preaching.* . . . To rise before the people to deal out common places which have cost you nothing, as if anything will do for a sermon, is not merely derogatory to the dignity of our office, but it is offensive in the sight of God. We must be earnest in the pulpit for our own sakes, for we shall not long be able to maintain our position as leaders in the church of God if we are dull. Moreover, for the sake of our church members, and converted people, we must be energetic, for if we are not zealous, neither will they be. It is not in the order of nature that rivers should run uphill, and it does not often happen that zeal rises from the pew to the pulpit. It is natural that it should flow down

---

[10] Dallimore, *Spurgeon*, 77.

from us to our hearers; the pulpit must therefore stand at a high level of ardor, if we are, under God, to make and to keep our people fervent.[11]

George Whitefield, the famed preacher of the eighteenth-century Great Awakening was also one who preached on his feet. Whitefield's sermons "show that he attempted first to reach the mind of the hearer, then to awaken his emotion, and finally to move his will."[12] These words mark the early ministry that continued on for George Whitefield. Encompassed in this classical focus of reaching the mind, the will, and the emotions of the listener, his zeal or earnestness came through in every letter, sermon, and prayer he expressed. It was written of Mr. Whitefield by one of those in attendance:

> The preaching of Mr. Whitefield excited an unusual degree of attention among persons of all ranks. In many of the city churches he proclaimed the glad tidings of great joy to listening multitudes, who were powerfully affected by the fire which was displayed in the animated addresses of this man of God. Lord and Lady Huntington constantly attended wherever he preached, and Lady Anne Franklin became one of the first fruits of his ministry among the nobility.[13]

These words show that a contemporary of the moment noticed how his "fire" and "animated address" played into

[11] Spurgeon, *Lectures to My Students*, 306.

[12] Arnold A. Dallimore, *George Whitefield: The Life and Times of the Great Evangelist of the Eighteenth-Century Revival* (Wheaton, IL: Crossway, 1990), 28.

[13] Ibid., 28, quoting *The Life and Times of the Countess of Huntingdon* (London, 1840), 1:20.

the overall effect on the hearers. It was Whitefield's earnestness that added to his greatness.

In an interesting side note, many offer the impact of Jonathan Edwards's sermon "Sinners in the Hand of an Angry God," which is purported to have been read aloud to the audience in a particularly monotone voice. The results of that sermon were deeply to affect the audience and break out a revival in that town of Enfield. Of course, historically speaking, Edwards is about the only example of this anyone can quote. But Edwards himself promoted Whitefield and specifically invited him to come to Enfield. Whitefield accepted the invitation and preached powerfully in that town. Edwards's response was described in Whitefield's own words as, "Preached this morning and good Mr. Edwards wept during the whole time. . . . The people were equally affected; in the afternoon, the power increased yet more."[14]

Earnestness, zeal, gusto, passion—all of these describe the same phenomena of one person with persuasion in mind, speaking from his heart with great energy so as to win the day for the cause.

Spurgeon gives us two final appeals on this topic of earnestness. He instructs us, "You must feel it yourself, and speak as a man who feels it; not *as if* you feel, but *because* you feel it, otherwise you will not make it felt by others."[15] He goes on to say, "Do try, as far as you can, to make the very way in which you speak to minister to the great end you have in view. Preach for instance as you would plead as you were standing before a judge, and begging for the life of a

[14] Ibid., 89, quoting Arnold Dallimore, *George Whitefield: The Life and Times of the Great Evangelist of the 18th Century Revival*, vol. 1 (Edinburgh: Banner of Truth; Westchester, IL: Crossway, 1980), 538.

[15] C. H. Spurgeon, *The Soul-Winner: How to Lead Sinners to the Savior* (Grand Rapids: Eerdmans, 1963), 98.

friend, or as if you were appealing to the Queen herself on behalf of someone very dear to you."[16]

Let's let Phillips Brooks conclude this section for us with this final challenge:

> The real power of your oratory must be your own intelligent delight in what you are doing. Let your pulpit be to you what his studio is to the artist, or his court room to the lawyer, or his laboratory to the chemist, or the broad field with its bugles and banners to the soldier; only far more sacredly let your pulpit be this to you, and you have the power that is to all rules what the soul is to the body. You have enthusiasm which is the breath of life.[17]

Preaching Essential 3: Personality

Persuasion and earnestness as we noticed before need a mode in which they can happen; a proper method, a proper process will make the difference. Reading a speech or using a thick set of notes perhaps can be persuasive, but it can only be earnest with great effort and probably some acting on the part of the speaker. The key to earnestness, which is the key to persuasion, is personality. No person is more persuasive than when expressing his own fire in his own way. Phillips Brooks is most famous for having written the Christmas hymn "O Little Town of Bethlehem," but his Yale lectures to students entering the ministry are perhaps his greatest enduring contribution. Brooks defined *preaching* in these lectures:

---

[16] Ibid., 100.

[17] Phillips Brooks, *Joy of Preaching* (Grand Rapids: Kregel, 1989), 134, originally published as *Lectures on Preaching*, 1877.

> *Preaching is the communication of truth by man to men.* It has in it two essential elements, truth and personality. Neither of those can it spare and still be preaching. The truest truth, the most authoritative statement of God's will, communicated in any other way than through the personality of brother man to men is not preached truth.[18]

Brooks went to great lengths to explain this insight, and at its core is common sense; God has given each individual his own personality, somewhat shaped by nature and somewhat shaped by experiences. Authenticity comes across when one speaks from his own person as guided by the Spirit of God. A preacher attempting to mimic someone else has the disadvantage of echo and the incongruity akin to a police officer giving directions in the high pitched voice of Mickey Mouse. Brooks displays this difference in describing the effect of two preachers:

> I think that, granting equal intelligence and study, here is the great difference which we feel between two preachers of the Word. The Gospel has come *over* one of them and reaches us tinged and flavored with his superficial characteristics, belittled with his littleness. The Gospel has come *through* the other, and we receive it impressed and winged with all the earnestness and strength that there is in him.[19]

---

[18] Ibid., 25.
[19] Ibid., 27.

Brooks adds, "Let a man be a true preacher, really uttering the truth through his own personality, and it is strange how men will gather to listen to him."[20]

Brooks' observation is undeniably true because the preacher who understands that he is a messenger, and the message comes through him, is the preacher who is in a position to speak with earnestness and persuade his hearers. Each of the sixty-six books of the Bible has a message from God, but the message is delivered through the uniqueness of each writer. When a preacher is free from notes and a written manuscript, the greatest possibility arises for his true personality, borne along by his true zeal, to allow for a persuasive message to be poured out through his soul. Rick Warren puts it in simple terms like, "If I don't feel it, I forget it."[21] Brooks clarifies that the uniqueness of *how* the truth is presented comes as the message through the messenger:

> No live man at any one moment is just the same as himself at any other moment, nor does he see truth always alike, nor do men always look to him the same; and therefore in his sermons there must be the same general identity combined with perpetual variety which there is in his life. His sermons will be all alike and yet unlike each other. And the making of every sermon, while it may follow the same general rules, will be a fresh and vital process, with the zest and freedom of novelty about it. . . . Establish this truth in your minds and then independence comes. Then you can stand in

---

[20] Ibid., 29.
[21] Rick Warren, *Church Growth Conference* (Lake Forest, CA: Saddleback Church, 1996), sound cassette.

the right attitude to look at rules of sermon-making which come out of other men's experience. You can take them as helpful friends and not as arrogant masters.[22]

Persuasion and earnestness will come through the uniqueness of the preacher's own style, voice, and personality as led and developed by the Spirit of God. This is certainly not about diligent preparation but about how a soul saturated with the truth delivers it to an audience. The use of the sanctified or Spirit-led personality means that the nature of preaching will take on a shape unique to the individual. There are always principles, there are always forms, there are always templates, but earnestness and persuasion come from the unique way a unique man of God pours out truth by God's leading and design. Once again carefully consider Brooks' words:

> I want to make you know two things: first, that if your ministry is to be good for anything, it must be your ministry, and not a feeble echo of another man's; and second, that the Christian ministry is not the mere practice of a set of rules and precedents, but a broad, free, fresh meeting of man with men, in such contact that the Christ that has entered into his life may, through his, enter into theirs.[23]

Koller adds the importance of freshness in the pulpit:

> Basic to all freshness in the pulpit is the demand that the preacher be himself, and not an imitator

---

[22] Brooks, *Joy of Preaching*, 114.
[23] Ibid., 88.

of others. Left to themselves, no two preachers
will develop the same sermon on a given text,
because no two preachers have exactly the same
intellectual endowments or the same background
of individual experience.[24]

History bears out and experience confirms that preaching which comes through the uniqueness of the preacher
offers the best sermons that that man can produce. This too,
as history attests, comes through a well-prepared heart in a
spontaneous, preaching on your feet style which gives the
best venting and the best possibility for the personality of the
preacher to be engaged. Brooks finally observed:

> The principle of personality once admitted
> involves the individuality of every preacher. The
> same considerations which make it good that the
> Gospel should not be written on the sky, or com-
> mitted merely to an almost impersonal book, make
> it also most desirable that every preacher should
> utter the truth in his own way, and according to his
> own nature.[25]

If we continue to write, use thick notes, take the seminary classroom into the pulpit, and, even worse, subscribe to
other preachers' sermons and read them as though they are
our own, we're not only doing damage to our current congregations, but we're setting the stage for the fine art of authentic preaching to disappear from the ranks of those leaders in
the generation ahead.

---

[24] Charles W. Koller, *How to Preach without Notes* (Grand Rapids: Baker, 1964), 1:102.

[25] Brooks, *Joy of Preaching*, 36.

Chapter 4

Advantages of Preaching on Your Feet for the Preacher and the Audience

*P*reaching on your feet is loaded with advantages. In fact, as I reflected on this area, it struck me that I finally must simply stop listing advantages. The value of this chapter is to convince, persuade, and comfort the person who has committed to preaching on his feet or who is seriously considering what this new approach might mean. Of course, it is also of value to lay out advantages so that naysayers are required to address why their objections overcome the advantages. It seems simple enough to list these advantages with a few comments.

Time Management

Time is perhaps the greatest advantage that preaching on your feet offers to the preacher. Not time preparation but the time saved in manuscripting and note-making. Preach-on-your-feet preparation turns out to be more about profound reflection after hard study than it is about notes and manuscripts. I, for example, preach about forty minutes in a regular sermon. I speak at a pace of about two hundred words a minute (perhaps even slower), and I can write somewhere between one thousand and fifteen hundred words an hour comfortably. All this to say somewhere between five-and-a-half to eight-and-a-half hours of my week will need to be taken up with writing a manuscript. Now, if my intention is to publish a text, perhaps this could be understood as valuable; but in the regular week of serving as a shepherd to people, a leader to staff, a father to five children, a husband to one wife (and the list goes on), then those eight hours become a pricey commodity. Moreover, it could be eight hours spent on better illustrations, better reflection, or deeper understanding of the text. There is so much to pastoral ministry. The methods by which we have enslaved preachers cause them to wear out and long for retirement. What a shame when the empowerment of preaching on your feet could return to them joy, energy, and rest for pastoral ministry without sacrificing the quality of the sermon.

Broadus adds an insight regarding the time spent in writing a sermon; these five to eight hours are usually hurried and the quality diminished because of all the demands of ministry. In quoting Wayland he writes:

> A large portion of written discourses is prepared in a driving hurry, late on Saturday night, and sometimes between the services on the Sabbath; and the thoughts are huddled together with little arrangement, and less meditation. If the same time had been spent in earnest thought,

would not the discourse have been more carefully prepared than by the simple process of writing?[1]

Connection with the Audience

One of the greatest advantages to preaching on your feet is the likelihood of connecting with the audience. Preaching is a life-to-life, spirit-to-spirit conversation. When a preacher develops the ability to organize his thoughts, own them in his soul, and pour them out directly to an audience, connection is all but inevitable. The reading of a manuscript or thick notes serves the same effect as holding up a manuscript and reading it in front of people. There's a break with the audience because, in particular, there's a break with eye contact. Alfred Gibbs describes this advantage with the following:

> He can then watch the effect of the sermon on the faces of his hearers. Thus the audience itself will aid him in his preaching. He can see the dawn of conviction upon this one, or that one. Sometimes he may actually be able to see conversion take place, as a person grasps the soul-emancipating truth of the finished work of Christ. The preacher's humble, but careful and prayerful preparation of the sermon is now rewarded, as he sees the interest shown and the blessed result from his message.[2]

Wayne McDill in *The Moment of Truth*, asserts:

---

[1] John A. Broadus, *A Treatise on the Preparation and Delivery of Sermons*, 23rd ed. (London: Hodder & Stoughton, 1898), 459; CD-ROM, Logos Research Systems, 1997.

[2] Alfred P. Gibbs, *The Preacher and His Preaching*, 6th ed. (Kansas City, KS: Walterick, n.d.), 227.

Eye contact is the most important element in non-verbal communication. When the preacher looks his hearers in the eyes, he makes contact with them in a way not possible otherwise. The eyes are the window of the soul. The audience can catch a better sense of the message through good eye contact, but they also catch a better sense of the preacher as a person.[3]

McDill goes on to describe the report of a preaching professor who counted the number of breaks of eye contact in a sermon he had been invited to evaluate on a Sunday morning. "He (the preacher himself) guessed maybe 20 to 25 times. He was shocked when told that his guest had 161 occasions when the preacher broke eye contact to look at his notes."[4] Beyond the issue of eye contact, the read sermon sounds read. Reading connects the audience and the manuscript, while speaking connects the audience to the speaker.

The Possibility of the Audience Remembering

One of the great and powerful benefits of preaching on your feet is that in order to keep the message in your own mind as a preacher, you tend to organize it in a way simple enough for your audience to remember. If you use elaborate notes, or a manuscript, your tendency will be to create such complexity that the response of the audience is to take notes (as though taking notes makes a difference in understanding). The truth is that if you can remember a sermon and deliver it to the people on your feet, they're

---

[3] Wayne V. McDill, *The Moment of Truth: A Guide to Effective Sermon Delivery* (Nashville: Broadman & Holman, 1999), 142.

[4] Ibid., 142.

going to remember it late into the week because it will be simple enough to recount to another person. Charles Koller offers dated but frequently verified information when he says, "Psychologists, conducting tests under laboratory conditions, have found that people remember that which is read to them, with forty-nine per cent efficiency. Retention increases to sixty-seven per cent when the thought is expressed, not by reading, but by direct address."[5] Koller references what common sense tells us: direct address is more memorable than being read to.

Finney underscores this fact:

> Now I have the best of reasons for believing that preachers of written sermons do not give their people so much instruction as they think they do. The people do not remember their sermons. I have in multitudes of instances heard people complain—"I cannot carry home anything that I hear from the pulpit." They have said to me in hundreds of instances: "We always remember what we have heard you preach. We remember your text, and the manner in which you handled it; but written sermons we cannot remember."[6]

The Example of Humility

Among the most powerful things we can do as preachers of the Word of God is to lead and influence by way of example. It is ubiquitous that the Greeks talked about ethos,

---

[5] Koller, *How to Preach without Notes*, 1:39, quoting John N. Booth, *The Quest for Preaching Power* (New York: Macmillan, 1943), 222.

[6] Charles G. Finney, *Memoir of Rev. Charles G. Finney: Written by Himself* (New York: Revell, 1876), 93.

pathos, and logos; the ethic, the emotion, and the logic in a complete presentation. The ethic, or character, had to do with the believability of the person speaking. The preacher who might on occasion stumble over words, imperfectly communicate a fact, or correct a mispronunciation actually conveys a humanness and a humility that shows his lack of perfection as a man stumbling in the right direction toward Christlikeness. Precision and perfection in sermon delivery only serve to communicate that the life the preacher lives is not obtainable by the people in the pew. Most manuscript readers sound "just right" and stuffy.

Adaptability

Preaching on your feet offers the ability to adapt to the circumstances around you. A few months ago as I was beginning my sermon in our second service, an individual had a heart incident which caused him to pass out. Quickly we were able to pray and sing a few choruses while the emergency medical team arrived to attend to this man. I then stood up with about ten minutes shaved off my sermon time; and yet, because I knew what I wanted to communicate, I was able, by God's mercy, to deliver a clear message, address the text, and stay on course. Adaptability can apply to babies crying or dramatic news that everyone has heard on the way to church. Preaching on your feet offers an adaptability that is unavailable to someone glued to his notes or staying the course with a written text.

Koller gives a historical example concerning adaptability: "On the Sunday following the attack on Pearl Harbor someone made the observation, in one of our large cities, that most of the sermon topics announced for the day gave no intimation that the preacher had even heard of Pearl Harbor, or was aware that our country had been plunged into war."[7]

Holy Spirit Led

This advantage will be discussed in detail later; however, there is a dependence on, and a possibility of, the Spirit of God leading in the midst of the sermon that is impossible with a thick outline or written notes. The hope for the manuscripter is that the Spirit of God was leading when the text was written because the Spirit has no room to lead during delivery. With a read sermon the Spirit can't say, "Stop." Instead, we tell Him, "Use this!" Gibbs describes this problem with the following:

> The speaker can accustom himself to think more rapidly and with less dependence on external helps. He can turn to advantage any fresh ideas that occur to him as he preaches, as led by the Holy Spirit of God. This will sometimes lift him unto an exaltation of mind that almost amounts to rapture, until he wonders where the words are coming from. Such an experience is better experienced than described.[8]

Of course, Gibbs is also addressing adaptability here; however, this experience of the work of God in the midst of delivery is an authentic, biblical, and important aspect of preaching. Those who manuscript are often scared to death of such

---

[7] Koller, *How to Preach without Notes*, 1:98–99.
[8] Gibbs, *The Preacher and His Preaching*, 227.

things; and yet in adaptability, in connection, in communication, in communication with an audience, an availability and a freedom for the Spirit of God to lead, though perceived as a risk, turns out to be a great advantage for authentic preaching on your feet.

Personality Trumps Plagiarism

Preaching on your feet gives the greatest opportunity for your unique individuality to come through. There's nothing more important than a preacher learning to preach in his own voice, in his own style. Warren and David Wiersbe put it well:

> This means the message God has given you, presented in the way he wants you to present it.
>
> Plagiarism has been defined as the lowest form of larceny and the highest form of compliment. Dean Inge called originality "undetected plagiarism." The faithful preacher will milk a great many cows, but he will make his own butter. Mark Twain was right: "Adam was the only man who, when he said a good thing, knew that nobody had said it before him."
>
> You need not document every truth or idea in your sermon that you picked up from your studies. But if you use another man's sermon outline, give him credit. If you quote an especially good statement, document it. Integrity demands it—and you never know whether somebody in your congregation might own the same book!
>
> If it is wrong to steal a man's material, it is also wrong to imitate his approach and style.

"The style is the man" said Robert Frost, and he was right. Be yourself—your *best* self—and let the Holy Spirit put the imprint of your life on the message. If another man's message has blessed you, then allow it to permeate your own mind and heart so that you can make it your own and apply it to the people. Lay hold of the essentials, not the accidentals.

Be yourself and be true to yourself. That is the best kind of originality.[9]

Preaching Becomes an Act of Faith

Of course reading a sermon, especially reading someone else's sermon, could be considered an act of faith, but there is nothing like trusting God with a soul saturated with the truth, a burden in a message, a feeling welling up of what you hope to communicate to an audience that has come to listen; and in that moment, having to trust God for the words and the clarity and the impact. Faith actually is the cutting-edge component of preaching on your feet. It is largely unavoidable for the preacher who reads to have faith in the written sermon rather than the living Spirit.

Growth in Confidence

Emerson supposedly observed, "The greater part of courage is having done it before." A kind of confidence continues to build, not in one's self, but in how God has honored and developed and grown you as a preacher. Week in and week

---

[9] Warren W. Wiersbe and David Wiersbe, *The Elements of Preaching: The Art of Biblical Preaching Clearly and Simply Presented*, CD-ROM, Logos Research Systems, 1997.

out you can arise with a clear understanding, with the words freshly arriving as you lay out the truth to the audience. This ongoing process of learning to be a "practiced thinker" allows a deepening conviction and availability of what may yet come because you have seen God steadily deliver you, and deliver to your audience, a truth from your heart to theirs without dependence on a refined strategy in the form of a written manuscript or cumbersome notes.

Readiness

As you grow in the skill of preaching on your feet, you're ready for more opportunities to preach. It is no wonder preachers actually preach so little nowadays without sermon quality being much improved. As you learn the skills and develop a new dependence on the Spirit of God to stand before people and communicate a thought clear in your mind, a truth clear in the Word but freshly in the moment, it is then that you can accept more invitations, that you can preach more often. There's a readiness for the moment as God develops you. It may be in a public meeting, it may be a sudden opportunity to preach a funeral, it may be an assembly at a Christian school; but in every event you're ready and available because you're not burdened with a need to spend an exhaustive amount of time "preparing a message" (or worse yet, digging an old one out of your cabinet, dusting it off, and hoping you can retool it for the need of the moment). If you don't know how to preach on your feet, then you cannot be ready until the manuscript is ready.

A Walk with God Is More Intimate to Preaching

Those who learn to preach on their feet actually learn that everything they study and everything they do in life becomes material for preaching. In particular, walking with God, spending time in His Word, abiding, listening, praying—all become means through which the soul is filled with truth and hope and insight. When the preacher himself becomes a part of the message, then everything the preacher does and studies and learns becomes a part of what he can share with an audience.

You Become Sharper (If Not Smarter)

The ongoing practice of profound reflection and study expressed in fresh and extemporaneous ways before an audience really develops the ability to think on your feet. This ability to think as you talk and reflect and clarify, even as the words come out, allows your brain to establish new connections and new skills and new abilities, such that you're constantly integrating and refining information. One example of individuals who have become smarter through this process is the trial attorney. These lawyers have had to learn to think quickly in negotiations and in the courtroom—and it comes by practice. Imagine the advantage to the preacher who learns to think in the moment, freshly and clearly. As Broadus put it, "This method teaches one to think more rapidly and with less dependence on external aids than if he habitually depended on a manuscript."[10]

---

[10] John A. Broadus and Vernon L. Stanfield, *On the Preparation and Delivery of Sermons*, 4th ed. (San Francisco: Harper, 1979), 270.

Fresh Delivery

Broadus also adds this advantage:

> In the act of delivery, the extemporaneous speaker has immense advantages. With far greater ease and effectiveness than if reading or reciting, he can turn to account his ideas which occur at the time. Southey says: "The salient points of Whitefield's oratory were not prepared passages; they were bursts of passion, like the jets of a geyser when the spring is in full play." Any man who possesses, even in an humble degree, the fervid oratorical nature, will find that after careful preparation, some of the noblest and most inspiring thoughts he ever gains will come while he is engaged in speaking.[11]

Broadus goes on to add another advantage in delivery: the sermon itself becomes warmer and more alive. He writes, "The whole mass of prepared material becomes brightened, warmed, sometimes transfigured, by this inspiration of delivery."[12]

Henry Ware adds:

> There is more natural warmth in the declamation, more earnestness in the address, greater animation in the matter, more of the lightning up of the countenance and whole mien, more freedom and meaning in gesture; the eyes speak, and the fingers speak, and when the orator is so excited

---

[11] Broadus, *Treatise on the Preparation and Delivery of Sermons*, CD-ROM.
[12] Ibid.

as to forget every thing but the matter on which his mind and feelings are acting, the whole body is affected, and helps to propagate his emotions to the hearer. Amidst all the exaggerated coloring of Patrick Henry's biographer, there is doubtless enough that is true, to prove a power and the spontaneous energy of an excited speaker, superior in its effects to anything that can be produced by writing.[13]

Whether because of the adrenaline of the moment, the leading of the Spirit, or the burden of the message itself, the individual who preaches on his feet has a huge advantage in delivery. The primary reason is simple: he is not acting. No matter the energy, love, and concern of the preacher who has written his sermon, his sermon is still "old"; it is an echo and requires an actor's talent for finding a way to seem freshly burdened in the moment. A man who reads well must engage a special knack to pretend he means the message as much in the reading as he did in the writing.

Joy in Preaching

Preaching on your feet offers a particular kind of joyful exhilaration that is largely unreachable by the person chained to notes. Spurgeon observed this fact when he wrote:

> Men who read borrowed sermons positively
> do not know anything about our troubles of mind
> in preparing for the pulpit, or our joy in preaching

---

[13] Henry Ware Jr., *Hints on Extemporaneous Preaching* (Boston: Hilliard, Gray, Little and Wilkins, 1831), chapter 1, http://www.prism.net/user/fcarpenter/warejr.html (accessed July 13, 2007).

with the aid of only brief notes. A dear friend of mine, who reads his own sermons, was talking to me about preaching, and I was telling him how my soul is moved, and my very heart is stirred within me, when I think of what I shall say to my people, and afterwards when I am delivering my message; but he said that he never felt anything of the kind when he was preaching.[14]

I'm sure there are exceptions, but the exceptions can't legitimately comment on joy until they have preached on their feet. In my own experience I know the difference between a sermon I've written and a sermon I've poured out through my soul; my audience knows the difference too.

The Audience Is Expectant

The audience is in view with all of these advantages, but there is a qualitatively different expectation when the preacher comes fresh each week and connects with the people. Professor Howard Hendricks observed a simple and profound fact to us during a class at Dallas Theological Seminary: "Gentlemen," he said, "as predictability goes up, impact goes down." The congregation most easily maintains a fresh expectation when a fresh message is brought weekly through a fresh preacher who preaches on his feet. If the manuscripted sermon is anything, it is a means of creating predictability.

---

[14] C. H. Spurgeon, *The Soul-Winner: How to Lead Sinners to the Savior* (Grand Rapids: Eerdmans, 1963), 98–99.

Chapter 5

What History Says about Preaching on Your Feet

*I*t has been said that "a precedent embalms a principle."[1] Looking back to our comments in the preface concerning Karl Barth, it may simply be that some preachers who used a written manuscript became the precedent that embalmed the principle. The truth of the matter is that there have been preachers of some renown who used manuscripts or thick outlines, but they have been the exceptions. In fact, until we had paper, the written outline or the written sermon was not actually much of a possibility for most speakers. Before the advent of easy-to-acquire paper, preachers and speakers simply used their minds, as did their audiences. Studies continue to appear which confirm what most of us know in our hearts, that the more notes we take, the less we listen. It is little wonder that excellent preachers are rare in our day and time. Between writing sermons and the audience's obligation to take notes,

---

[1] Quote attributed to British Prime Minister Benjamin Disraeli, ThinkExist. com Quotations, http://en.thinkexist.com/search/searchquotation.asp?search=pr ecedent+embalms&q.html (accessed April 2, 2006).

few of us are talking from our heart or listening with our heads because we are all busy with our notes.

The purpose of this chapter is to display that the true standard has always been preaching on your feet. The fact that history is on the side of preaching on your feet leads to four simple insights.

Prominent Speakers Spoke on Their Feet

History's famed speakers, both secular and Christian, were individuals who spoke extemporaneously. The record of history shows that the overwhelming majority of speakers spoke on their feet. Many others, whom we assume wrote or used notes, may indeed not have done so at all. Often excellent speakers will carry some information with them but hardly refer to it at all. This happened when Martin Luther King Jr. stood to declare before the masses, "I have a dream!" Most assume that he shared a well-crafted and well-organized speech written and refined.[2] The facts, however, tell a different story. Dr. King had been mulling over the ideas involved in the "I Have a Dream" speech for about two weeks, dating back to a point when it crossed his mind in Detroit. The truth is that he read about five sentences of a prepared speech and put it aside; the remainder of the "I Have a Dream" speech was extemporaneous, without notes. Dr. King was preaching on his feet. The language, the passion, and the words were all in that moment created by a man who had learned to be what Spurgeon called a "practiced thinker."[3]

---

[2] Ken Howard, who argued persuasively against writing speeches, assumes that Dr. King's speech was written. Ken Howard, *Act Natural: How to Speak to Any Audience* (New York: Random House, 2003), 89. Reviewing the film clip of the speech shows Dr. King setting his notes aside.

[3] C. H. Spurgeon, *Lectures to My Students* (Grand Rapids: Zondervan, 1954), 149.

Human Nature Hasn't Changed

Preaching on your feet today can find support in history because the nature of human beings has not changed. In our age we're fond of speaking about culture as though it is the driver; in reality human nature is the true driver, and it gives rise to culture. Human beings have always found the most effective and popular speakers to be those individuals who speak directly to them in plain language with passion and clarity. Preaching on your feet is the simplest and most direct path to communicating effectively within the boundaries of human nature. The power of direct communication is transcultural because it is the direct path to the human heart.

You Are Not Alone

If you want to learn how to preach on your feet or pursue a unique style through the principles involved in preaching on your feet, then it will serve you well to know that you are not alone. You have the most famous voices in Christian history on your side, supporting you; regardless of denomination or orientation, the famous Christian speakers have overwhelmingly been individuals who learn to speak on their feet.

Preaching on Their Feet Probably Explains Why They Were So Successful

I pose this possibility for our reflection. Some individuals have a greater measure of God's grace in their gifting (see Rom 12:3), but preaching on their feet may have been the strategic element that unleashed their gift. If we could go back as good scientists and really perform the experiment, we would force these individuals to preach from a manuscript.

We can't of course do that, but I believe that we would destroy or greatly minimize the impact of these individuals with manuscripts. Essentially, history tells us that preaching on their feet was a part of their charm, a part of their power, a part of what engaged their earnestness as preachers. I believe history screams to us that any man who preaches well with a written manuscript or a thick set of notes will preach even better if he learns to preach on his feet.

An Honor Roll of Extemporaneous Speakers

The remainder of this chapter is designed to overwhelm you with the support of historical evidence that the best orators, sacred and secular, have spoken extemporaneously. Preaching on your feet is the historically proven means by which the greatest speakers had the greatest impact. An excellent source of information on this subject is David L. Larsen's *The Company of the Preachers*, which I highly recommend.[4]

John Chrysostom (c. 347–407), patriarch of Alexandria, is recognized as the greatest preacher of the ancient church. He became known as Chrysostom (the golden mouthed) because of his eloquence. Many of his sermons are in print and merit careful study, but they were originally delivered extemporaneously. Larsen explains, "Often he carried on what seems to be a dialogue with his congregation, with question and response. He preferred his ambo, or pulpit, rather than the bishop's throne, because it was closer to the people. He was sometimes criticized for being too dramatic."[5] Yet Chrysostom was an amazingly biblical preacher for the times, who studied, and

---

[4] David L. Larsen, *The Company of the Preachers: A History of Biblical Preaching from the Old Testament to the Modern Era* (Grand Rapids: Kregel, 1998).
[5] Ibid., 83.

reflected, and then poured out his heart in common terms and in direct interaction with his audience.

Augustine (354–430), though better known as a theologian, was also an effective preacher. And like Chrysostom he spoke extemporaneously. His sermons are still in print and are carefully studied by preachers today, but they were originally delivered extemporaneously and stenographically recorded. Larsen explains:

> We have 685 of his sermons, some of which consumed an hour and some of which were very brief. He was sparse with illustration but fond of pithy aphoristic sayings, loved rough Punic words, and was noted for his logic and rhetorical devices such as alliteration and rhyme. He explained and repeated the text, although he was guilty of horrendous misinterpretations on occasion. His delivery had striking beauty and affect.[6]

Martin Luther (1483–1546), the father of the Reformation, was a monk before breaking with the Roman church, but he continued his life of prayer after becoming a Reformer. His conviction of the centrality of Scripture led him to preach biblical sermons though he sometimes strayed from his text. He was the most effective preacher of his day, and his sermons are still in print, but Luther delivered them extemporaneously.

The Swiss Reformation broke out in Zurich under the leadership of *Huldrych Zwingli* (1484–1531). Although his sermons were not recorded, he is known to have preached extemporaneously. Larsen describes his method:

---

[6] Ibid., 90.

Zwingli's sermons would begin with the reading of the biblical text, then a wrestling with its meaning with adaptation to the hearers and their situation. He used homely illustrations and borrowed from the classics. He loved farm illustrations we might consider crude and made artful use of humor as a bridge to reach his audience.[7]

After Zwingli's death, *John Calvin* (1509–1564) became the Reformer of the French-speaking city of Geneva, Switzerland. Like Luther, he preached regularly, and his expositions were recorded by a stenographer. These were published as biblical commentaries, and they are still studied widely by preachers and other Bible students. Larsen explains:

During Calvin's four years in Strasbourg when he pastored the French church, he preached nearly every day and twice on Sundays. Until he died, the pulpit was the heart of his ministry. When summoned back to Geneva in 1541, he resumed his exposition on the next verse from the place where he had stopped. The pattern of preaching twice on Sundays and in alternate weeks at a daily evening service continued in Geneva. He preached extempore, that is, without a manuscript. (Calvin faulted the English for using manuscripts.)[8]

Cotton Mather (1663–1728), the leading Boston preacher of his day,

---

[7] Ibid., 174.
[8] Ibid., 166–67.

would preach for at least an hour, often an hour and three-quarters. Once his pastoral prayer went for two hours, and he had to apologize. He did his exegesis and outlining in the typical Puritan form and valued illustrative anecdotes to help his audience get the picture. He spent considerable time internalizing his message because he neither read from a manuscript nor memorized his sermon. He typically took about seven hours for preparation. He spoke in free style, extempore.[9]

John Wesley (1703–1791), principal organizer of the Evangelical Revival in Britain and founder of Methodism, was once forced to resort to extemporaneous preaching when he lost his manuscript. Soon he adopted preaching on your feet as his standard method, though he and his brother Charles also published a standard set of sermons that are still widely regarded.

George Whitefield (1714–1770) was born in England and was, for a time, closely associated with John Wesley. Like Wesley he was an itinerant preacher, often preaching out of doors. He toured the American colonies, and his preaching did much to spark the First Great Awakening. Benjamin Franklin was so amazed at Whitefield's oratory that he included in his *Autobiography* a spell-binding description of Whitefield's preaching in Philadelphia—a must-read for every preacher.[10] He has been called America's first celebrity.

---

[9] Ibid., 300.
[10] *The Autobiography of Benjamin Franklin*, Harvard Classics (New York: Collier, 1909), 1:103.

Dallimore observes, "He had a most peculiar art of speaking personally to you in a congregation of four thousand people."[11] Another observer remarks:

> He made them laugh, he made them moan, he swayed them like reeds in the wind. A surly old general who despised preachers followed the crowd, listened as the young preacher described a blind man stumbling nearer and nearer to the edge of the precipice, forgot himself and preacher-hate and shouted right out in the meeting, "Good God, he's over!"[12]

According to Clarence Macartney:

> It goes without saying that Whitefield, the great field preacher, preached without notes. No man could have held the multitudes that he drew if he had read his sermon. No man who reads a manuscript can be heard by great multitudes like the man who lifts up his head and pours out the message from his heart. Whitefield's least effective sermons were those which he wrote early in his ministry. Now and then—but not often—he would go apart with those three still good friends, Adam Clark, Matthew Henry, and Cruden's *Concordance* and meditate for a season. He always claimed that the best preparation for preaching was preaching

---

[11] Larsen, *The Company of the Preachers*, 371, quoting Arnold A. Dallimore, *George Whitefield: The Life and Times of the Great Evangelist of the Eighteenth-Century Revival* (Wheaton: Crossway, 1979), 482.

[12] Ibid., 371, quoting Frank S. Mead, "The Story of George Whitefield," *The Sword of the Lord*, January 31, 1992, 3–4.

itself. There is much in that. Most of us do not preach often enough, and we have a tendency to develop a stilted, artificial manner when we do preach. Whitefield expressed great regret when his failing health put him on what he called "short allowance"—once every day and three times on Sunday. Benjamin Franklin, who delighted to hear Whitefield, thought that his written sermons and the published sermons gave no intimation of the preacher's great power.[13]

Whitefield offers us one of the great contrasts with the manuscript preaching style of the day, and his popularity and influence had to be tied to the way his passion was expressed because he preached on his feet.

John Newton (1725–1807), the Anglican clergyman and famous writer of "Amazing Grace," was also a high-impact preacher. His extempore preaching attracted many to his London parish. Eventually Newton lost his eyesight, but his blindness did not silence him because he had mastered the art of preaching on his feet.[14]

We have already quoted *Lectures to My Students* by *Charles Haddon Spurgeon* (1834–1892). Clarence Macartney reports:

> When Theodore Cuyler visited Spurgeon late one Saturday afternoon, that preacher with the marvelous voice told him that he had not yet selected a text for the next day's sermon, but that presently

---

[13] Ibid., 163–64.

[14] J. D. Douglas, Philip Wesley Comfort, and Donald Mitchell, *Who's Who in Christian History* (CD-ROM) (Oak Harbor, WA: Logos Research Systems, 1997).

he would go down into the garden, choose a text for the morning and evening, and then outline the morning's sermon. Sunday afternoon he would make an outline of the evening sermon. Spurgeon never composed a sentence in advance and spent little time laying out the plan of the sermon.[15]

Charles G. Finney (1792–1875) saw five hundred thousand professions of Christ in his ministry.[16] According to the historian Mark A. Noll,

a good case can be made that Finney exerted a more significant influence on American life, and certainly on American religion, than such other key figures as the essayist Ralph Waldo Emerson, the political statesman Daniel Webster, the educational reformer Horace Mann, and the historian Henry Adams.[17]

His preaching was extempore and sometimes impromptu, "throwing manuscripts away."[18] In his own words, "In delivering a sermon in this essay style of writing, the power of gesture and looks and attitude and emphasis is lost. We can never have the fullness of the gospel till we throw away our written sermons."[19]

Although expository preaching is not commonly associated with preaching on your feet, the pioneers of mod-

---

[15] Ibid., 162.

[16] Earl E. Cairns, *An Endless Line of Splendor: Revivals and Their Leaders from the Great Awakening to the Present* (Wheaton: Tyndale, 1986), 129–36.

[17] Mark A. Noll, *A History of Christianity in the United States and Canada* (Grand Rapids: Eerdmans, 1992), 176–77.

[18] Larsen, *Company of the Preachers*, 500.

[19] Ibid.

ern expository preaching spoke extemporaneously. *John A. Broadus* (1827–1895), whose classic textbook *On the Preparation and Delivery of Sermons* has been continuously in print since it appeared in 1870, was an eloquent defender of preaching on your feet. Another pioneer of expository preaching in the modern world was the Scottish pastor Alexander Maclaren (1826–1910), remembered for his published *Expositions*. According to Larsen, "The sermons we read were preached extempore and transcribed as he preached them. They seldom required editing. 'Burn your manuscripts,' he counseled preachers."[20] Similarly the famed London expositor *G. Campbell Morgan* (1863–1945) spoke extemporaneously.

George W. Truett (1867–1944) was another legendary preacher who spoke without notes. During his forty-five-year pastorate of the First Baptist Church in Dallas, Texas, he led the struggling congregation to become a thriving congregation of nine thousand members. According to Koller,

> During the latter half of his ministry he was away from his own pulpit about half the time; he "belonged to the world"; but the spiritual impact of his ministry kept the church life in high momentum to the very end. Those who heard him could scarcely imagine his preaching otherwise than without notes.[21]

James Buckley presents an overwhelming list of history's greatest secular orators, all of whom spoke on their

---

[20] Ibid., 581.
[21] Charles W. Koller, *How to Preach without Notes* (Grand Rapids: Baker, 1964), 1:37.

feet, including Quintilian, Pericles, Plutarch, Aristides, Themistocles, Demonsthenes, Cicero, Henry St. John Bolingbroke, Charles James Fox, Daniel O'Connell, John Bright, and William Gladstone.[22]

Buckley's list also includes some of America's most famous orators. You may be surprised to know that *Patrick Henry* never wrote a line of his speeches.[23] *Daniel Webster* usually wrote or thought out in sentences his set orations; but his pleas in court, many of his addresses in the Senate, and most of those on the platform were extemporaneous.[24] *Stephen A. Douglas* and *Abraham Lincoln*, whose 1860 debates changed the course of American history, had one thing in common: both spoke extemporaneously.[25]

And a growing number of contemporary preachers are recovering this classical approach. Most recently Andy Stanley and Lane Jones have offered an excellent work on communication that includes a persuasive explanation of why notes hurt communication.[26]

---

[22] James M. Buckley, *Extemporaneous Oratory for Professional and Amateur Speakers* (New York: Eaton & Mains, 1898), 343–78 passim.

[23] Ibid., 379.

[24] Ibid., 382.

[25] Ibid., 397.

[26] Andy Stanley and Lane Jones, *Communication for a Change: Seven Keys to Irresistible Communication* (Sisters, OR: Multnomah, 2006), 52.

Chapter 6

What the Bible Says about Preaching on Your Feet

*T*his chapter is the most difficult chapter to write in this entire book. It's difficult for two reasons. First, arguing principles from the Bible turns out to be an effort in frustration. For every person who names one principle from the Bible, there's another who will counter with either a different principle, or proof that that first principle is wrong. So when we speak of principles for preaching, we've opened, unfortunately, a can of worms.

In one of my last classes at Dallas Theological Seminary, we had an assignment to discern principles of disciple-making from the life of Christ. My friend Dr. Keith Bower and I, in an unguarded moment, spent a little time with the idea of "principles" and came up with a few additional disciple-making principles from the life of Christ. For example:

1. Spend a lot of time at the lake with your disciples.
2. Make sure your disciples are away from their families most of the time in the process of being discipled by you.

3. If a disciple disagrees with you, rebuke him and call him "Satan" to his face.

I believe you get the idea.

The second reason this chapter is difficult to write is that the Bible so singularly supports preaching on your feet that arguing to the contrary looks foolish.

Four basic points arise as we look at God's Word.

The Point: No Example to the Contrary

The point of this chapter is that the Bible has no example of any preacher ever using notes or a manuscript in his sermon. Though letters were read, there is no example of someone reading a sermon to an audience. Every biblical example of the preacher is an example of preaching on your feet, and yet it is necessary for me to emphasize this point in order to embolden people with the biblical authority so that they might be courageous in learning to preach on their feet.

The Distinction: 100 Percent Counter Examples

Both preaching and writing were available and understood in Bible times. Paper, or papyri, was probably not available in abundance, so writing out sermons or a thick set of notes had limited appeal. Of course, God providentially could have made paper available had He thought notes and manuscripts were necessary for bringing His message to any particular audience.

Take a moment to look under the entries for *preach* and *write* in a concordance, Bible search engine, or Web site. Then focus particularly on 1 Tim 3:15: "But if I am delayed, I write so that you may know how you ought to conduct yourself in the house of God, which is the church of the living God, the pillar and ground of the truth." Paul is writing to Timothy for the simple reason that he wanted Timothy to have information that would not be available if Paul was delayed. In other words, if Paul was not delayed, he would not have written. Why? Because if Paul had told Timothy, he would have used spoken words. The distinction to appreciate is that Bible writers and the speakers understood that writing was one thing and speaking was another. In their understanding there was no relationship between the two such that it was important to write what you were going to say before saying it, or particularly saying what you were going to say before you write it. This is perhaps the most fundamental misunderstanding in homiletics and preaching courses in our day.

The Rhetorical Burden: Writing Is Not Speaking

Any cursory study of the Old Testament or New Testament preachers will show that they preached on their feet. These details lay the rhetorical burden at the feet of those who insist that writing manuscripts or carrying into the pulpit a thorough set of notes is necessary for effective preaching. Those who insist on manuscripts and notes need to explain why it is a superior process, even though there are no examples of it being followed or encouraged in the entire Word of God. There is no example of an individual using notes or a manuscript to preach. All examples—100 percent—are of those who preached without notes. Writing was seen as an activity distinct from preaching; writing had a very distinct purpose as found in examples such as Col 4:16: "Now when this epistle is read among you, see that it is read also in the church at the Laodiceans, and that you likewise read the epistle from Laodicea." Letters were seen as something to be read, and the activity itself was understood as an activity distinct from the actual preaching of the Word of God. Another example is found in Acts 13:27: "For those who dwell in Jerusalem, and their rulers, because they did not know Him, nor even the voices of the Prophets which are read every Sabbath, have fulfilled them in condemning Him." Every Sabbath the voices of the prophets were read. But no one considered that to be the sermon or the teaching. The text was read, and then comments were made without notes and on their feet.

The Spirit's Role: Unencumbered

Consider Luke 12:11: "Now when they bring you to the synagogues and magistrates and authorities, do not worry about how or what you should answer, or what you should say. For the Holy Spirit will teach you in that very hour what you ought to say." Surely no one would suggest here that this is a pattern for all preaching, but it does indicate that God seems comfortable in certain circumstances for the preacher or speaker simply to trust the Spirit of God. Trusting the Spirit of God to bring clarity and burden is an act of faith and is clearly within the boundaries of what the Word of God teaches. Perhaps a greater dependence on the Spirit of God in combination with devout study could offer a new level or opportunity for the Word of God to go out to your audience with freshness and power.

Given these four points, the true rhetorical burden is clearly on those who claim that notes and manuscripts are necessary and important for the preacher. Let them attempt to prove it while those who dare trust God and preach on their feet carry on with the confidence that their activity is biblically sound.

The Wrong Question

The promoter of manuscripts and notes would probably at this point be asking, "Does the Bible ever say, 'Don't use notes'?" or, "Where does the Bible say, 'You must speak extemporaneously and without notes or manuscript'?" Of course this kind of question is mistaken in its form. Questions themselves can be designed to elicit a particular answer. It is common in college rhetoric classes to throw out an old and unfair question, "Are you still beating your wife?" I was taught in school to take that question and say, "It's not a fair question since I never did beat my wife. Would you like to rephrase it?"

To go to the Word of God and say that its silence to any exact point proves the point is to drift away from a clear discussion. What exactly is the Bible trying to tell us? To ask, "Does the Bible say it's wrong to use notes?" we must answer, "No." If we were to ask, "Is the use of notes and manuscripts unsupported biblically?" we would have to say, "Yes!" Perhaps a follow-up question would be, "Is it biblically right to use notes?" and in this case, we would simply say, "No, there is no support for using notes." In all of these cases we can arrange questions to support our desired result.

The Right Question

The right question is, What does the Bible say about this subject? This question doesn't seek to go beyond what the Bible says, and it doesn't seek to create conclusions from what the Bible is silent about. The right question is something in the following direction: *Are you following the biblical pattern when you preach on your feet?* It is not so much the concern here that using manuscripts or notes is wrong, but, rather, that *it is blatantly appropriate to preach on your feet.* When I say, "Biblical pattern," I mean the overall, consistent way in which the Bible exemplifies and explains any particular issue. Church government, for example, shows that the biblical pattern is a church led by a plurality of qualified elders. This statement does not attack other forms of government, but rather it is to say that if indeed a church has a plurality of qualified elders, that church is following a (the) biblical pattern, which in ecclesiology simply means that to argue that elder-led churches are unbiblical is actually to have to argue against the pattern.

When we ask, "Are you following the biblical pattern when you preach on your feet?" the answer is a resounding yes. Every example of preaching in the Word of God involves preaching on your feet.

The Conclusion of the Matter

The conclusion of the matter is that the individual who seeks to preach on his feet can do so with profound confidence that the Word of God is without question fully supportive in such an activity. Second Timothy 2:15 gives one piece of the conclusion of the matter, "Be diligent to present yourself approved to God, a worker who does not need to be ashamed, rightly dividing the word of truth." It is clear that study and hard work are priorities for the preacher, and yet later in the same book Paul writes to Timothy, "Preach the Word! Be ready in season and out of season. Convince, rebuke, exhort, with all longsuffering and teaching. For the time will come when they will not endure sound doctrine, but according to their own desires, because they have itching ears, they will heap up for themselves teachers" (2 Tim 4:2–3).

We are instructed to preach the Word and to preach sound doctrine and to do so as a result of much study; but our readiness is to be in season and out, in any circumstance, in any situation. I don't believe I go too far when I say, be ready with notes or without, convince, rebuke, exhort, with all longsuffering and teaching.

Perhaps the most incredible passage in the Word of God on the difference between writing and speaking is found in 2 John 12: "Having many things to write to you, I did not wish to do so with paper and ink; but I hoped to come to you and speak face to face, that our joy may be full." John, in writing his epistle, simply exposes the contrast in his mind concerning paper and ink versus face-to-face. Maybe he's not speaking of preaching, but maybe he really is. Indeed it may be that a preacher is simply having a one-on-one conversation with a large group of people when he preaches. Naturally, there's oratory, style, voice, and so forth; and yet preaching on your feet is about this face-to-face communication that is biblically distinct from the use of paper and ink. Be confident that when you preach on your feet the Bible is on your side.

Chapter 7

_____

Reflections on Thought and Language

*I*n its most simple form, preaching can be described as the use of spoken words to create thoughts in the listener. In many ways there's nothing more to it than that. It's amazing that we preachers stand before people and simply use sounds to generate thoughts, which generate feelings and actions, which cause lives to change. None of this is to deny the role of God, and yet God Himself was the one who created language for us and called us to speak forth as the oracles of God (1 Pet 4:11). Another way to think about preaching is that God has certain thoughts, and the preacher is endeavoring to think the same way God thinks about a particular subject. After getting himself to think the same way God thinks about the subject, the preacher then goes before an audience and uses words to get the audience to think like the preacher thinks.

Wendell Phillips succinctly explained, "'The chief thing I aim at is to master my subject. Then I earnestly try to get the audience to think as I do.' Even his great lectures, such as 'The Lost Arts' and 'Daniel O'Connell,' though carefully prepared, were never written out."[1] In biblical terms, as far as thinking goes, it is much as Paul said in 1 Cor 11:1, "Follow my example, as I follow the example of Christ" (NIV).

This issue of thoughts and language is strategic if you are ever to be freed to preach on your feet. Permit me to offer a somewhat unrelated example to stress this point. In a private conversation with Marsh Fisher, cofounder of Century 21 Real Estate and developer of the brainstorming software *IdeaFisher*, Marsh shared his basic understanding of problem-solving: *"The solution to any problem is just an idea."*[2] In this assertion, Mr. Fisher is inviting us to understand that when a problem is solved, the actual key to solving the problem is an idea, which then is later implemented.

I remember coming home many years ago while my wife, Jody, was decorating for Christmas. As I stepped into the kitchen, there was a line of brass candle holders with candles laying on their sides, charred on the bottom. As I looked at the candles, Jody said to me, "I know you know how to do this, but I can't get these candles to stay on these brass holders." What she had been attempting to do was heat the bottom of the candle with a lighter in order to soften it and place it on the brass candle holder spike. I looked at them and looked at her and said, "I think you need to heat the brass." Of course, the idea of heating the brass worked, and the candles have continued to stay in place throughout every Christmas season.

---

[1] James M. Buckley, *Extemporaneous Oratory for Professional and Amateur Speakers* (New York: Eaton & Mains, 1898), 404.
[2] Marsh Fisher, interview by author, Midland, TX, July 2004.

Lest you think this principle works only in the direction of me to my wife, consider another situation. One day I observed a conflict between one of our children and a friend who had come over to play (both were probably about four years old). These two individuals were beginning to fight over a toy, and I was about to step in and tell my child to share with his friend. Jody had the solution to the problem in a simple idea. She took the item and looked at these two little children and said, "Well, obviously you're both not old enough to play with this." And she placed it on a top shelf. I've watched her down through the years apply that idea so that whenever two children begin to fight over an item, she just puts it up. Well, before long our kids and any visiting kids learned how to cooperate if they wanted to keep an item in play.

In your problem-solving do you seek the idea that is the solution, or do you tinker around with what to do? I offer this illustration to show two simple things: (1) You gain an insight because you can now think like Marsh Fisher thinks; and (2) The actual words Marsh Fisher gave us generated the insight regarding problem-solving: "The solution to any problem is just an idea."

Think in Pictures, Think in Words

It is common these days for everyone to claim the high value of thinking in pictures. In fact, it is often said that we humans think in pictures. And true, we certainly do think in pictures; we can imagine a scene and describe it to someone. But the curious thing is that we actually think in words as well. There are at least two processing systems. Our children learn a great number of vocabulary words in our homeschooling practices. The two oldest boys find this rather easy because they can look at the words a number of times and memorize them relatively quickly to pass the test. My daughter does not process written information that easily; we realized this from just being observant parents. Laura was taking days and days to learn vocabulary words that the boys might learn in a few hours, so what were we to do? Thank goodness we knew that we think with more than just pictures, so we suggested to Laura to read her vocabulary words aloud to herself (she strikes us as an especially "auditory learner"). In no time, Laura was learning the words almost as fast as the boys.

The truth is, humans think in both pictures and words. After my studies in English literature at the University of Alabama, I attended law school for about a year. When I was accepted, my dad, who was an attorney, gave me *Black's Law Dictionary* as a congratulatory present. In the front of this dictionary, in kind words of congratulation, Dad wrote this phrase, "Verba sunt animo indices," which he translated, "Words are the indices of the mind." Words are the things that thoughts are made of. Words are the way we catalog and categorize and organize our understanding. *The most essential idea in this chapter is simply that words actually precede the thoughts.* Consider for example, children. As they grow and develop, we teach them words; and in the course of time, they can use these words to understand thoughts. It doesn't work the other way around.

Four Observations

Several basic observations come together to offer authentic freedom to the person desiring to preach on his feet.

1. You Can't Know before You Know.

Obviously we can't know before we know, but we miss the importance of this on most occasions. When we do not have knowledge, we simply do not have knowledge; and we cannot have knowledge before we actually have knowledge. The gibberish I'm speaking of would solve a lot of problems practically and theologically in our lives if we embraced this fact. Many of my hyper-Calvinistic friends make this same kind of mistake when they conclude that the elect are saved when they're elected by God before the foundation of the world. Of course, you can't be "saved before you're saved" anymore than you can know before you know.

If God elects an individual before the foundation of the world, then that person is chosen by God before he exists. Of course, a person cannot be saved unless he or she exists; therefore, we can know for a fact that a person is not "saved before she's saved," that is, no one is saved simply because he or she is chosen by God.

The Bible makes this point abundantly clear as well when it states in Eph 2:3, "Among whom also we all once conducted ourselves in the lusts of our flesh, fulfilling the desires of the flesh and of the mind, and were by nature children of wrath, just as the others." Paul is saying that there is a time in a person's life when he or she is by nature a child meant for wrath, but that in the mercies of God, He delivers us when we put our faith in Him alone (Eph 2:4–9). One is not saved before he's saved, nor can you know before you know. So why is such a point so important for learning to preach on your feet? Because when you stand before people to preach, you actually cannot know what you're going to say before you say it.

This currently overlooked fact that you can't know what you're going to say before you say it is the exact reason most people gravitate to preaching with manuscripts and notes. In truth parents and educators have contributed to this problem with simple instructions like, "Think before you speak." The intention with such a phrase is to invite someone either to be clear or careful before he opens his mouth to ramble. In that sense, it's wise to consider your words. But it is important to slow down your thinking and communicating process enough to notice that you actually cannot know what you're going to say before you say it.

I'm sure you as a reader at this point in the conversation are greatly questioning my sanity and this proposition, but you can prove it to yourself by simply paying attention to how conversation goes between you and another person. You do not know what you're going to say. You may have some idea, some direction, some thought; but your exact wording and the exact pieces are only rarely in your mind. This is one of the strange things about introverts, who want to think before they speak; they, indeed, run into the problem of trying to figure out everything they're going to say so that they can say it correctly, so they don't get into trouble or cause a problem or conflict in the interaction.

Unfortunately, the tendency is to try to formulate the words in your head before you say them. In truth, people can only pull a few words together in that kind of sequence before it gets confusing. Yes, you can memorize; yes, you can practice telling a joke enough times to know basically how you're going to say it; but in the moment the actual words that are coming out and being formed were not consciously known beforehand. Here's another way to prove it to yourself: watch how you write. When you write a letter or a paragraph or a note to someone, you don't actually figure out the words first in your head, but rather you get the idea and then you get in motion putting the words down. Writing has the advantage of being able to be edited before you finally hand the written information to someone else. When we speak, we must edit as we go.

2. Words Create the Thought.

The pied pipers of postmodern Pabulum are attempting to convince us that our traditional ways of interpreting (the science of hermeneutics) spoken and written words are governed by whatever the listener wants the words to mean. In many ways it is preceded by modernistic thinking or by the orientation of the days of the judges: "everyone did what was right in his own eyes" (Judg 21:25).

I remember the question Mrs. Murphy used to ask our high school English class when we studied Shakespeare or Shelley: "What does it mean to you?" This idea has invaded our Bible study so that we're not interested in what the text means or what the author intended but simply what it means to you. The interpreter reigns supreme.

A common joke reveals this misunderstanding of thought and language. Jokes put together words in such a way that they create a reaction of laughter or amusement in the listener. Jokes, however, are dependent on the listener's actually "getting" the joke. For example, in the classic movie *Mary Poppins*, there is a dialogue in which one person says, "I knew a man with a wooden leg named Smith," and the respondent says, "Really, what was the name of his other leg?" This joke is not given to different interpretations; it's not given to phrases such as "What does it mean to you?" You either get the play on words, or you do not. When you go to McDonald's and order a Big Mac, the person taking your hamburger order can't ask, "What does Big Mac mean to me?"

When I say that "the words create the thought," I mean that the words in relationship to one another—normally we would call this the grammar—generate a meaning that is stable and solid. Of course you can have sentences or phrases that are ambiguous, but they still mean something ambiguous in a particular direction. If I said, "The dog is king," then I would mean that the dog reigns in the place of a king in some imaginary story or perhaps that the dog is the king of the home and is the thing around which a family organizes all activities. Changing the word order actually changes the meaning, so that if I say, "King is the dog," then the relationship of those words generates the meaning that King is referring to his name, not necessarily his status.

Preachers in particular are fond of stressing the importance of authorial intent, or what the author meant to communicate. In the Bible this is a valid interest because we're trying to get at what an infallible God meant to communicate through His infallible Word. In our common, everyday language or in our preaching, this takes on a slightly different form. We might intend to say one thing and yet misspeak. "Please hand me that knife," you might say, pointing to the pen in your spouse's hand. He or she would probably look at you with confusion. You, still hearing your own words hang in the air, realize that you used the word *knife* instead of *pen*. Your next step is to adjust and say, "Oh, I mean, *pen*." The reason you can know that you misspoke is that words create the thought. Although you intended to ask for the pen, the words you used created a different meaning for your spouse.

3. Thought Calls Forth Words.

This observation gets to the heart of how we communicate and specifically how we can learn to preach on our feet. In communicating you can have an intention even though the exact wording is not decided upon before you speak. I play a little game with my students (I tutor writers) in order to stress this principle. The game is simply that we have something we intend to say, such as, "The queen is beautiful." With that in our minds, each student in the circle contributes the next word, so by the time we get through the sentence may look like, "The queen, named Zanderil, has the face that brings light like an angel in a dungeon." Of course, it may not turn out to be great writing, but the fact remains that the sentence itself could not preexist, since each student contributes a separate word. The intention guides the nature of choosing the words, but the words themselves, in the order they occur, create the actual thought.

Concerning preaching on your feet, Buckley weighs in on this point:

> It is frequently asserted that a speaker should attend primarily to thought, and that then language may be trusted to take care of itself. This is true with respect to a particular effort about to be made; but since, with the possible exceptions previously noted, there can be no thought without mental root words or signs, and every word, the meaning of which is understood, deposits a thought in the mind at the same instant that it embeds itself in

the brain, the acquisition of language is the acquisition of ideas and facts under such circumstances that ever afterward the thought will suggest the word and the word the thought.[3]

Buckley is observing the intimate nature of language and thought. The words create the thought, but the thought calls forth the words, and this insight can change everything for you if you want to be one who preaches on his feet.

4. You Can Prepare by Thinking Out Loud.

The relationship of these observations leads us to understand the fact that language and thought are intimately connected in such a way that they follow the basics of the creative process. In the creative process you begin with some vision or thing you wish to create (e.g., beef stroganoff). You next look at what you have available (Is there beef in the refrigerator?) and work out a plan. Each step in the plan is taken, and then evaluated, with some adjustment likely made (you may be leaving for the store, but your neighbor calls, and in the conversation mentions that she has plenty of beef for you to borrow).

Putting together words follows a similar process. You begin with some intention in terms of a thought that you hope to communicate. Next you pick a word and add another word, evaluate how those words are beginning to form or communicate the thought, make adjustments, and add more words. The amazing thing is that since you have been designed by God for language, this use of sounds happens at the speed of light.

This means through which you communicate with people daily is the same means through which you can communicate

[3] Buckley, *Extemporaneous Oratory*, 34.

when you preach on your feet. *The most powerful thing you can do in preparation is to think out loud.* Naturally, thinking on paper can work pretty well too, but the idea is to work through your understanding with the use of phrases with the explanations that come as you openly discuss the various points you hope to communicate with your audience. The power of feeling and earnestness also comes through this process.

Buckley states, "A refined and often the most impressive way of making one's feelings known is merely to describe them."[4] You can easily see this happen in counseling or in discussion with an upset child by simply asking her to tell you how she feels. As a person describes his or her feelings, the words create the thoughts, and the thoughts spark the feelings. This same thing happens when you are preaching on your feet: having the intention of explaining something you're passionate about, beginning to choose your words as you share them with your audience, they in turn generate thoughts for the audience and yourself, which gives life to feeling and earnestness, which cannot but come through in your mannerisms, in your voice, and in further thoughts that they are thinking along with you and the feelings they're experiencing through your use of words.

The Point

The point in learning to preach on your feet is to learn to have confidence by casting off a misunderstanding about language and thought. After preparing, praying, and reflecting, thought and language simply bring forth this one powerful truth: *If you know what you intend to say, then the words will come if you start.*

---

[4] Ibid., 35.

Chapter 8

The Master Keys to Preaching on Your Feet

*I*n his famous allegory *Pilgrim's Progress,* John Bunyan describes how the giant Despair captures Christian and places him in a stinking dungeon. As they were losing all hope, Christian and his companion pray through the evening; suddenly Christian remembers that he has a key, called Promise, in his pocket. This key opens the way of escape from the dungeon.

Life itself is loaded with keys, and much like Christian we can find keys in things we do; some of these keys are unnoticed. Any good Bible student knows that the key to interpretation is careful observation of what the text truly says. From observing Ephesians 5, any good husband can understand that the key to a healthy marriage is a love that produces safety for his wife. Any good wife can see from the same passage that respect is the key that leads to joy in marriage for her husband. Students who attend college finally discover that the key to success is simply to go to class and do each day's lesson. We might consider any number of keys to preaching on your feet, but two are especially important and make the difference in learning this art. The keys to preaching on your feet are *learning* and *exclusivity*.

Consider Buckley's words when he first entered the ministry:

> Before entering college I determined to study law, and accordingly took great interest in debate, in attending courts, and in reading accounts of cases. But young men frequently change, and a few years later I had become a minister, and was obliged to make choice among different methods of public speaking. After experiments with all I adopted the extemporaneous, and ever since have systematically practiced and studied this art.[1]

Buckley understood both of these principles—learning and exclusivity—and at the outset affirmed them to his readers. He understood that he must actually learn how to preach, and second, that he must give himself entirely to the method to be learned.

Master Key 1: Learning

Preaching on your feet must be learned. One would think it goes without saying that something such as an approach to preaching must be learned; but we tend to think that certain people are endowed naturally without learning being involved. The story is told of a traveler who came to a small village and asked a man sitting at the village entrance, "Any famous men born in this village?" The man puffed on his

---

[1] James L. Buckley, *Extemporaneous Oratory for Professional and Amateur Speakers* (New York: Eaton & Mains, 1898), v.

pipe, thought for a second, and looked at the traveler before saying, "No Sir, just babies." The truth is that we all start out as babies. No matter our gifting and talents and privilege, things truly must be learned. Mozart had to learn the scales. Einstein had to learn math. Shakespeare had to learn to form his letters.

What is learning? And at what point can we say something is indeed learned? Over years of reflection, I've decided that the easiest way to understand learning is with the phrase, "Speed of access." By "speed of access" I mean the speed at which a person can draw upon information or skill. Speed of access defines whether information or skill has been learned. For example, if someone has memorized a fact, such as a phone number, then the nature of learning suggests that if the individual can instantly recall the phone number, we can indeed say she has learned it. On the other hand, if with much struggle, sorting out the numbers and finally getting the number correct happens, but with great labor we cannot safely say it has been learned. Someone who dabbles or is in the process of learning something does not yet have the speed of access that comes when something is truly learned. The same principle applies to a skill; a skill suggests the ability to do it, an ability actually to carry out the actions necessary to produce the desired results.

Preaching on your feet is a skill that must be learned, not a natural endowment that begins at the first attempt. Missing this point is probably the reason so many have attempted but quit the process of learning to preach on their feet. Consider Macartney's observation on this point with regard to George Whitefield:

Preaching without notes is by all odds the hardest way, both as to preparation and as to delivery. Whitefield, who is one of the pioneers in preaching without notes, was attacked on this ground by professors at Harvard who declared that no strong argument could be handled convincingly without a manuscript. Whitfield answered: "Indeed, gentlemen, I love to study and delight to meditate. Preaching without notes costs as much, if not more, close and solitary thought, as well as confidence in God, than with notes." There's no doubt about that. It takes more out of a man, both in preparation and in the preaching. Let no minister choose this method for any reason except that experience proves it to be the most effective.[2]

Macartney is not simply pointing out that the method requires hard work but also that this hard work must be engaged in before the result of preaching on your feet is ever reached.

Finney weighs in on the need for preaching on your feet to be learned by saying:

For I am still solemnly impressed with the conviction, that the schools are to a great extent spoiling the ministers. Ministers in these days have great facilities for obtaining information on all theological questions; and are vastly more learned, so far as theological, historical, and biblical learning is concerned, than they have perhaps ever have been in any age of the world. Yet with

[2] Clarence Edward Macartney, *Preaching without Notes* (Nashville: Abingdon Cokesbury, 1946), 145–46.

all their learning, they do not know how to use it. They are, after all, to a great extent, like David in Saul's armor. A man can never learn to preach except by preaching.[3]

Finney's words ring true in this century as much as they did in his own. Schools are great mechanisms through which individuals are prepared, and students acquire many skills related to theology and the study of God's Word. But Finney's statement that "a man can never learn to preach except by preaching" is as straight as it gets. An individual who learns to preach reasonably well using manuscripts and thick notes does so by actually preaching with manuscripts and thick notes. Though obvious, it stands to reason that in order to learn to preach on your feet, you the preacher must learn how by being engaged in the process of learning how. Finney goes on to clarify and emphasize his point:

> Now I never had a thought of undervaluing the education furnished by colleges or theological seminaries; though I did think, and think now, that in certain respects they are greatly mistaken in their modes of training their students. They do not encourage them to talk to people, and accustom themselves to extemporaneous address to the people in the surrounding country, while pursuing their studies. Men cannot learn to preach by study without practice. The students should be encouraged to exercise, and prove, and improve, their gifts and calling of God, by going out into any

---

[3] Charles G. Finney, *Memoir of Rev. Charles G. Finney: Written by Himself* (New York: Revell, 1876), 88.

place open to them, and holding Christ up to the people in earnest talks. They must thus learn to preach. Instead of this, the students are required to write what they call sermons, and present them for criticism; to preach, that is read them to the class and to the professor. Thus they play preaching.[4]

Finney, as president of Oberlin College, is not criticizing the value of education, but he is certainly stating that common ministerial education can be improved. Preaching, and by that he means preaching on your feet, cannot be learned by mere study; it must indeed be practiced. The artificial nature of writing a sermon and reading or presenting it in a classroom is not preparation for ministry where ministry occurs: outside the walls of the seminary or Bible college. The very idea that preparing a manuscript and reading it, let's say, to a group of professors, and thereby calling it preaching, is ludicrous. If we defined preaching in the way scholars approach it—that is, to carefully manuscript a thorough treatise on a tedious theological point, followed by reading the manuscript to the audience—then I dare say Christianity, as we've ever known it, would end in no time. The direct address of heart-to-heart communication is the essence of preaching on your feet, and that direct address is learned by directly addressing people who live out in the common day-to-day world.

Spurgeon adds his two shillings to the importance of learning in his lecture called "The Necessity of Ministerial Progress":

---

[4] Ibid., 89–90.

First, dear brethren, I think it necessary to say to myself and to you that we *must go forward in our mental acquirements*. It will never do for us continually to present ourselves to God at our worst. We are not worth His having at our best; but at any rate let not the offering be maimed and blemished by our idleness.[5]

Spurgeon understood that there is a constant and ongoing learning process in all aspects of ministry. Preaching itself is certainly not an exception, no matter the gifting. Diligence means we begin where we begin, and we learn to do a little better. Spurgeon adds to the importance of learning the following: "When you are able to feel at home in the pulpit, and can look round and speak to the people as a brother talking to brethren, then you will be able to extemporize, but not till then."[6] Obviously, no one begins by feeling at home in the pulpit and free to speak as a brother to brethren. Preaching in such a style, and indeed in such a relaxed style, is something that comes with age and time and labor. Preaching on your feet, preaching at ease in the pulpit, is obtainable; but it is obtained through learning. Spurgeon adds: "*Every man who wishes to acquire this art must practice it*. It was by slow degrees, as Burke says, that Charles Fox became the most brilliant and powerful debater that ever lived."[7]

Finney offers our final thought on the nature of learning and courage:

---

[5] C. H. Spurgeon, *Lectures to My Students* (Grand Rapids: Zondervan, 1954), 205.
[6] Ibid., 151.
[7] Ibid., 149.

In our school at Oberlin our students have been led—not by myself, I am bound to say—to think that they must write their sermons; and very few of them, not withstanding all I could say to them, have the courage to launch out, and commit themselves to extemporaneous preaching. They have been told again and again; "You must not think to imitate Mr. Finney. You cannot be Finneys."[8]

Finney understood the importance of involving the individual's personality in preaching, and he understood that preaching on your feet is the means through which the personality is released or engaged in preaching. His critics dismissed Finney as an exception. Finney, perhaps, was an exception, but the exception in Finney was not his giftedness but his courage. His call to everyone who wishes to learn how to preach on his feet is simply to launch out courageously. There indeed is the starting place, if not perhaps the essence, of what learning anything truly takes.

Of course, writing itself is no cure for the concern some have for extemporaneous preaching. As Charles Koller notes: "Writing out the sermon in full does not necessarily insure accuracy of expression. There is much extemporaneous writing as well as extemporaneous speaking. And hasty, slipshod writing may be more harmful than beneficial to style."[9]

The first master key is that you must accept the truth that preaching on your feet must be learned and then strike out courageously learning it.

---

[8] Finney, *Memoir*, 91.
[9] Charles W. Koller, *How to Preach without Notes* (Grand Rapids: Baker, 1964), 1:88.

Master Key 2: Exclusivity

Preaching on your feet must be exclusive. I believe this particular master key is the hardest thing in this book to accept. It is often our hope and wish that we can create an easy transition in learning a new skill. But much like swimming, transition doesn't come unless you're in the water. Swimming is not learned by studying a book alone, nor is it learned by making swimming motions in your living room. In order to learn to swim, you must get in the water. The principle of exclusivity is a principle that says the preacher must give himself wholly to this method.

Spurgeon alludes to the importance of exclusivity by offering the way to learning this art is by including the practice in one's day-to-day life:

> Conversation, too, may be of essential service, if it be a matter of principle to make it solid and edifying. Thought is to be linked with speech; that is the problem; and it may assist a man in its solution, if he endeavors in his private musings to think aloud. So has this become habitual to me that I find it very helpful to be able, in private devotion, to pray with my voice; reading aloud is more beneficial to me than the silent process; and when I am mentally working out a sermon, it is a relief to me to speak to myself as thoughts flow forth.[10]

Spurgeon already tells us the means through which we can begin learning to preach on our feet, and that is, to begin to

---

[10] Spurgeon, *Lectures to My Students*, 149.

speak on our feet, to form the habit of speaking while alone, reading aloud, and reflecting aloud on the things we're reading. He adds:

> Good impromptu speech is just the utterance of a practiced thinker—a man of information, meditating on his legs, and allowing his thoughts to march through his mouth into the open air. Think aloud as much as you can when you're alone, and you will soon be on the high road of success in this matter.[11]

It is not so much that Spurgeon is thinking here that we must exclusively preach on our feet in the pulpit but rather that our lives be dominated by the process and the processing involved in thinking aloud.

Macartney underscores the importance of exclusivity or single focus from his own experience:

> I recall my own experience when I went out at the end of my junior year in the seminary to a picturesque little village in Wisconsin. I had my first sermons well in hand, but had copious notes on the pulpit Bible. I did not refer to the notes, but the fact that they were there chained me, as it were, to the pulpit. After a few Sundays had passed, I abandoned the manuscript altogether and launched out into the great deep of preaching without notes. Since then I have never preached

---

[11] Ibid., 149.

either with a manuscript or with any notes what-
soever in the pulpit.[12]

This is indeed what is meant by *exclusivity*. It is a single-
minded commitment and a single-minded focus on learning fully, intimately, and finally how to preach on your feet.
Finney goes on for pages in his autobiography explaining the
importance of this single-minded focus, this exclusive commitment to preaching on your feet. In that process he draws
his readers' attention to the beginning place of exclusivity:

> But unless men will try it, unless they will
> begin and talk to the people, as best they can,
> keeping their hearts full of truth and full of the
> Holy Ghost, they will never make extemporane-
> ous preachers. I believe that half an hour's ear-
> nest talk to the people from week to week, if the
> talk be pointed, direct, earnest, logical, will really
> instruct them more than the two labored sermons
> that those who write, get off to their people on the
> Sabbath.[13]

Preaching on your feet begins with an exclusive commitment
to master this approach, beginning as Finney says, "as best
they can" in endeavoring to preach directly to people with
the truth in the heart.

Spurgeon vividly underscores the importance of this
master key of exclusivity:

> If you are happy enough to acquire the power
> of extemporary speech, pray, recollect that *you*

---

[12] Macartney, *Preaching without Notes*, 160.
[13] Finney, *Memoir*, 95.

may very readily lose it. I have been struck with this in my own experience, and I refer to that because it is the best evidence that I can give you. If for two successive Sundays I make my notes a little longer and fuller than usual, I find on the third occasion that I require them longer still; and I also observe that if on occasions I lean a little more to my recollection and my thoughts, am not so extemporaneous as I have been accustomed to be, there is a direct craving and even an increased necessity for pre-composition. If a man begins to walk with a stick merely for a whim, he will soon come to *require* a stick; if you indulge your eyes with spectacles they will speedily demand them as a permanent appendage; and if you were to walk with crutches for a month, at the end of the time they would be almost necessary to your movements, although naturally your limbs might be as sound and healthy as any man's. Ill uses create an ill nature. You must continually practice extemporizing, and if you gain suitable opportunities you should frequently speak the word in cottages, in the school-rooms of our hamlets, or to two to three by the wayside, your profiting shall be known unto all men.[14]

Spurgeon is applying the principle from Galatians 6:7 to preaching on your feet. Paul states it simply, "As you sow, you shall also reap." Beginning with some extemporizing is fine; but a full commitment to learn, and in every opportunity

---

[14] Spurgeon, *Lectures to My Students*, 152.

and in every situation, to begin to fully depend on the abilities God handed you as you study hard, think profoundly, and share authentically on your feet—that is the means through which this art is mastered. Any dabbling with notes and manuscripts invites a greater dependency on notes and manuscripts. Macartney offers this final exhortation:

> But whatever method the preacher decides to employ, let him give himself wholly to it. Let him preach with the conviction that it makes the greatest difference in the world whether he does his work well. Let him speak to the souls of men, realizing that they are created by God and fitted to hear the Word of God, and let him expect that the soul will respond to the voice of God. Let the preacher remember that he is speaking to souls who are at the parting of the ways, and for whom this may be like John's great "tenth hour," when he who hears may see and find the Lord.
>
> And always let him preach God's message with a warm heart. This was the prayer that was so often upon the lips of George Whitefield, that great hunter of souls—"O Lord, grant me a warm heart!"[15]

Macartney's exhortation to "give himself wholly to it" is the essence of this second master key. Preaching on your feet must be exclusive; it must become your style, your way, your method, your heart—only in that decision will it finally be learned and mastered.

---

[15] Macartney, *Preaching without Notes*, 171.

Chapter 9

Preparing to Preach
on Your Feet

*I*n preparation, nothing should shine so bright in the preacher's mind and heart as the thought of Woodrow Wilson: "Where there's a fire, thither will men carry their lamps to be lighted."[1] Or the words of Longfellow: "To me, a sermon is no sermon in which I cannot hear the heartbeat."[2] The fire and the heartbeat in a sermon are formed in the preparation, not in the moment. If a preacher is to preach with earnestness and intensity, with fire and heart, then he must acquire the burden of the message in the preparation. For he who would preach on his feet, all of life is preparation. But here we mean the more specific work of the preacher concerning the message, the Word of God, and how to approach communicating to a specific audience. Buckley summarizes the best practice for preaching on your feet: "Extempore speeches in debate, premeditated as to their main points, and impromptu replies depending wholly upon

---

[1] Ralph L. Lewis, *Persuasive Preaching Today* (Ann Arbor, MI: LithoCrafters, 1979), 21.
[2] Ibid.

the demands of the occasion, jointly form the best method of practice."[3] Indeed, this is the most useful and simple explanation of how to prepare, including what delivery involves. There is, decidedly, premeditation as to main points, as to information, as to insights, as to illustrations; and yet, as the occasion arises and the audience is before the preacher, then the impromptu or extemporaneous selection of words with earnestness—these combine to give birth to a message for a moment in time.

In the beginning efforts of learning to preach on your feet, your temptation will be to memorize great portions or strategic portions of the message; but when preparation has been effective, being carried along in the moment as you rise before an audience will be your standard experience. Buckley adds this promise of the joy of learning to preach on your feet: "After a short experience the stimulus of being dependent upon the working of one's own mind without the aid of intentional recollection will be found worth more than any drug which effects the nerves, more than any influence of human origin."[4]

François Fénelon gives us the most "comprehensive and precise" description of the extemporizer, the one who preaches on his feet:

> He is a man who is well instructed, and who
> has a great facility of expressing himself; a man
> who has meditated deeply in all their bearings
> the principles of the subject which he is to treat;
> has conceived that subject in his intellect and has
> arranged his arguments in the clearest manner;

---

[3] James M. Buckley, *Extemporaneous Oratory for Professional and Amateur Speakers* (New York: Easton & Mains, 1898), 413.
[4] Ibid., 425.

has prepared a certain number of striking figures
and touching sentiments which may render it sen-
sible and bring it home to his hearers; who knows
perfectly all that he ought to say, and the precise
place in which to say it, so that nothing remains at
the moment of delivery but to find words in which
to express himself.[5]

Essentially, Fénelon is telling us that if we are well prepared, then delivery is simply a matter of rising and finding
the words as they're needed. It is in this sense that preaching on your feet is an animated conversation but a conversation resulting from careful study and profound reflection.
My intention is to give you, the reader, some idea of how
to go about preparing to preach on your feet. Although the
most strategic things I can say will come toward the end of
this chapter, it is important to understand what preparation
is about in order to appreciate the most strategic way to prepare. We will examine the three elements of preparation: (1)
solo style, (2) saturation, and (3) single focus.

Element 1: Solo Style

Solo style refers to the fact, even the imperative, that every
preacher must develop his own style of preparation, of reflection, and of delivery. Until he develops his own solo style, he
will have limited freshness and earnestness in his message and
limited impact on the audience. Charles Koller reminds us:

Basic to all freshness in the pulpit is the demand
that the preacher be himself, and not an imitator

---

[5] Quoted in ibid., 429.

of others. Left to themselves, no two preachers will develop the same sermon on any given text, because no two preachers have exactly the same intellectual endowments or the same background of individual experience.[6]

The preacher's own individual approach to study and reflection and labor is the key to preparation.

One of the most powerful things you can do is to write your own book on how you prepare your sermons. You may not write the book to share it with others, but having written, you will certainly have more clarity on your own approach. I have come to realize that I can study a book or a topic in any order I wish, but my mind can still go back and put it in an order that the subject needs. I often will chase different passages that relate to the topic and different words in a passage only to return and reorder my thoughts around the structure of the verses. I also like to arrive at tentative conclusions on my own before I read the commentators. Others may find reading commentaries to be more helpful at the beginning to get a frame on the debate about a passage before wrestling it through themselves. The preacher is a chef, not a server in a lunch line. He must learn and grow in his own unique approach to sermon preparation.

Element 2: Saturation

For one who would preach on his feet, nothing is more important than saturation. In saturation the soul is being soaked in the topic at hand. Once thoroughly saturated like a

---

[6] Charles W. Koller, *How to Preach without Notes* (Grand Rapids: Baker, 1964), 1:102.

sponge, you need only be squeezed out on Sunday morning. Koller underscores the importance of saturation while at the same time prophetically challenging the growing practice of simply preaching bought sermons:

> Whatever method of preparation the preacher may follow, he needs to be thoroughly familiar with his material. He must know the subject and all its ramifications. "No man can be eloquent on a subject that he does not understand," as Cicero, the greatest orator of ancient Rome, declared two thousand years ago. Even inspiration cannot work in a vacuum.
>
> The preacher must not begrudge the time spent in gathering his factual data and preparing his Scripture analysis on the way to his sermon outline. "It is a general principle that anything which costs the producer little is of little value to others." One of the penalties of plagiarism is that it so largely bypasses the process of saturation.[7]

Saturation is the key to authentic, high-impact preaching. Study and reflection is to cost the preacher something. A manuscript or notes become unnecessary when a preacher is truly saturated, that is, when a preacher truly understands his subject and the passage at hand. Koller suggests his own approach to preparation, given his emphasis on saturation: "A good procedure is to select a sermon topic early; meditate

---

[7] Ibid., 1:85. The first quote is from Wilbur E. Gilman, Bower Aly, and Wilbur Reid, *Speech Preparation* (Columbia, MO: Artcraft, 1946), 29. The second quote is from Wilson T. Hogne, *Homiletics and Pastoral Theology* (Winona Lake, IN: Free Methodist Publishing, 1940), 31.

upon it daily; let the sermon grow; then write the outline in one sitting."[8]

In summary, saturation is any number of means through which you, in your own individual style, can immerse yourself in a text or in a topic you wish to bring before an audience, observing the text, debating the text, having friends discuss the topic with you, reading commentaries, reading books, listing as many questions as come to mind about a text—all of these can be means through which a preacher saturates himself as preparation. Any means of immersion that you find helpful becomes a satisfactory path through which you're fully soaked in the subject.

Element 3: Single Focus

Whether one chooses the saturation with planned structure or the saturation with unplanned structure approach, it is important to keep in mind, and to communicate clearly, one primary idea. Webb states this point in forceful terms:

> Homiletically there is some debate about the need for a bottom-line statement, a single sentence, as it were, that sums up everything in the sermon. When one is talking about preaching without notes, however, there is no debate. Parenthetically, it is my view that the habit of writing out and reading full sermon manuscripts in the pulpit— manuscripts that are essentially essays, however fluid their style—is largely responsible for our having lost sight of the importance of having a

---

[8] Ibid.

single, well defined statement around which the entire sermon is well constructed.[9]

Even the most elementary student can see that Jesus had a point in each of His parables. Preachers have turned the parables into many points and subpoints, but Jesus was aiming at one clear message. The person who seeks to preach on his feet and connect heart to heart with his listeners is well served by deciding on *the* point as the basis for organizing his long study, preparation, and saturation in the truth at hand. With these three elements in view, saturation can now be seen strategically in its planned and unplanned forms.

Saturation with Planned Structure

In preparation for preaching on your feet, saturation and focus can be enough, but most preachers still learning how to preach on their feet find it valuable to have structure to the message. Structure, of course, is the relationship that exists between various elements. A bookshelf has a structure related to vertical and horizontal planes; an outfit has structure in the relationship of colors and patterns from scarf to shoes. The same idea is important for the preacher. Among the most helpful questions is simply, "How will I communicate with this audience?" In this sense, structure is related to how exactly the audience will be approached. Some preachers enjoy following the structure of a passage itself. And so, in an overview of a book like Ephesians, a clear break occurs between chapter 3 and chapter 4; the first half of the book is dealing with the high calling of the saint in the Lord while the second half of the

---

[9] Joseph M. Webb, *Preaching without Notes* (Nashville: Abingdon, 2001), 46.

book is concerned with walking worthy of that high calling. Depending on the nature of the event, the topic, and the passage, any number of structural approaches can be useful and valuable. None of them, however, should diminish the importance of the meaning of the text. When a preacher has a structure in his mind, finding the words to explain the structure becomes a ready and reachable task. Perhaps the easiest way to approach structuring a sermon, and the process of soaking and preparing, is to use templates.

A template is basically a form into which different information can be poured and easily organized. The following are a few examples of templates that can be used to create a structure *after* thoroughly soaking on the material for the message.

1. The Problem-Solution-Action Template

The problem-solution-action template is an excellent approach for both secular and sacred situations since problems are a part of the universe. This approach addresses the problem; explains how the Bible or passage at hand, or a truth concerning the nature of God, solves the problem; and, finally, offers a specific action to take. For example, Philippians 4:8, which describes the importance of keeping our thinking on things that are good, pure, lovely, and the like, can easily fit this template. The problem to address before the congregation could concern a question such as, What do we do with our bad feelings and worries in our day-to-day life? The first part of this template—the *problem*—could be developed by expressing how much people worry, the kinds of worries they have, and the origin of these worries based on news reports and speculations from newscasters. People are tempted to find solutions, even though many problems are genuinely unfixable; so the real solution is to fix our own thinking. The *solution* is to develop the discipline involved in keeping our thinking on the kinds of things described in Philippians 4:8. Finally, the *action* to take: focusing on one item in the Philippians 4:8 list, such as "praiseworthy," could lead to the action of finding one praiseworthy thing and spending one day focused on it. Examples could be offered according to different aspects of life: relationships, work, business, politics, friendship, and family. It's easy to see how a template can organize information, but it is important to recognize that the preacher should not begin with a template, but rather with full immersion in the text or the topic. The template then comes along as an opportunity to organize or structure the information into a message for the audience.

2. The Tension-Seeking-Resolution Template

Robert Fritz explains this principle thoroughly as it relates to business, filmmaking, and works of fiction.[10] In fact, Fritz would argue that all of life is involved in these tension-seeks-resolution structures. In a tension-seeks-resolution template the idea is to begin with the end in mind. What is the resolution or the answer that the passage or the truth offers the audience? It may be the simple gospel message, that according to John 3:16, one can be fully assured he or she has eternal life because of faith in Christ. Full assurance, that settled promise found throughout the Word of God, is the place at which the sermon ends. Therefore, much like stretching a

---

[10] Robert Fritz, *The Path of Least Resistance: Learning to Become the Creative Force in Your Own Life* (New York: Ballantine, 1989). Fritz as the originator of Structural Dynamics has trained thousands of professional creators and is a mentor to Peter Senge of the Sloan School of Management of Massachusetts Institute of Technology (MIT).

rubber band in order to create the tension structurally for the sermon, you would think of the opposite of where you hope to end. In this case, the resolution is salvation, eternal life, and assurance; the beginning spot, therefore, would be the opposite, or a place of condemnation, doubt, and foreboding. It would be a matter of shooting straight about the path in which those who have not yet trusted Christ find themselves if they look around, a path that is surely heading them to an eternity separated from the joy found in a relationship with the living God. With this tension established, each step in the sermon would begin to resolve the tension; the direction toward destruction might next be met with the fact that paths can be changed, then next by the fact that God created a different path, then by the fact that Jesus Christ is the doorway through which the new path is found, now that faith in Christ and His redeeming work is the mechanism through which the door is open and the new path is begun; and the final resolution, the challenge to believe in Christ. This template works from establishing tension and then ending with resolution.

3. The Key Words Template

Simply organizing a message around key words in the passage, or key words for communicating the passage, has been found by many to be a very helpful approach.

4. The Personal Persuasion Template

The template of personal persuasion asks and answers three questions:

1. What does it say?
2. What does it mean?
3. What convinced me, the preacher, personally?

I've preached on the doctrine of election with this type of template, where my final appeal and my own understanding is what convinced me concerning the fact that God wrote my name in the Book of Life before time began; which gives Him all of the glory in the salvation process compared to the other views which give glory to man.

5. Inductive Bible Study Template

Howard Hendricks, in *Living by the Book*, influenced by Robert Traina's *Methodical Bible Study*, offers three and four basic stages in understanding a passage.[11] Each of these asks and answers a question:

1. What does it say? (Hendricks/Traina)
2. What does it mean by what it says? (Hendricks/Traina)
3. Where does it fit? (Traina)
4. What difference does it make? (Hendricks/Traina)

These questions work from observation to interpretation to correlation (where is the topic discussed elsewhere in the Bible) to application (how do I use it in my life?). This template is an easy and effective way to walk a congregation through a passage toward understanding and application.

6. Strategic Questions Template

Although any template of valuable questions can be an effective approach, six questions have proved time and time again to be an effective way to approach any subject. The

---

[11] Robert A. Traina, *Methodical Bible Study: A New Approach to Hermeneutics* (New York: distributed by Biblical Seminary in New York, 1952); Howard G. Hendricks and William D. Hendricks, *Living by the Book* (Chicago: Moody, 1991).

questions are, Who? What? When? Where? Why? and How? As a template, walking through these questions can be a powerful way to explain a passage or a truth to an audience.

7. Monroe-Motivated-Sequence Template

Another template is a pattern developed by Alan H. Monroe. This professor at Purdue University organized simple steps in a persuasive process that can be effective in organizing or structuring a message.[12]

1. The Attention Step: getting attention
2. The Need Step: showing the need
3. The Satisfaction Step: satisfying the need
4. The Visualization Step: visualizing the result
5. The Action Step: requesting an action

8. The Lybrand Template

This template is a modified Monroe Sequence, based on my own experience, which I have found effective in communicating with people. Here are the steps:

1. Engage the audience.
2. Expose their need.
3. Make a "contract" to meet that need in the message.
4. Explain the text: its meaning, implications, and illustrations.
5. Clarify: putting together the meaning of the text and how it meets the need of the audience.
6. Offer actions to take.
7. Close with a point-on illustration.

---

[12] Raymie E. McKerrow et al., *Principles and Types of Speech Communication*, 15th ed. (Boston: Allyn & Bacon, 2003), 180–205.

This combines the tension-seeks-resolution template with other templates we've seen above. You are invited to discover and catalog various templates or ways to approach structuring a message. Invent your own, experiment, but feel encouraged to structure your message after saturation.

Saturation with Unplanned Structure

Saturation with unplanned structure is the way most of us write letters. We think about our basic idea or point we hope to communicate through the letter. Next, we start. In this version of preaching on your feet, there is much less energy spent on trying to remember or organize an exact strategy. Instead, due to saturation and "owning" the subject, a speaker with skill in preaching on his feet weaves together all the reflection in an ordered and persuasive way. This aspect of preaching on your feet comes with later mastery; nonetheless, it is probably the highest form and most powerful way in which a preacher can impact a congregation in the moment. Of course, it involves much soaking and much preparation, but the words and the strategy arrive with the preacher in the moment he stands before the audience. The practiced thinker still has structures in his own understanding, and the text itself gives rise to structure. But given the situation, the preacher's own frame of mind and heart, and his years of experience in preaching, everything comes together in a Spirit-led, high-impact way that doesn't beforehand fit any template.

My Recommended Method

In 1898 James Buckley told of his discussion with a gifted preacher who read his sermons from a manuscript:

To encourage him I said, "In conversation you are one of the best extemporizers I ever heard; many a time I have known you to utter passages born of the moment which, if spoken in the pulpit, would raise your standing in the estimate of the most admiring auditor."

He made a set argument to prove that he could not extemporize in public, again demonstrating that his chief need was confidence. To contribute to this I said, "If you will follow the suggestions that I will give you, in six weeks from to-day you will speak to your congregation extemporaneously, with a force and fervor which will cause them to beseech you never to read another sermon."

He consented to make the trial, and the prescription was this: "During your summer outing in the mountains accept the first invitation given you to preach in a schoolhouse. Select a thing with which you're familiar, one that stirs your own heart, and has had an intimate relation to your deepest experiences. Meditate upon it, take a large view, mark out some grand divisions, ignore details, think only of what will illustrate your thought—not with the purpose of using any particular illustration, but of filling your mind with appropriate similitudes. Then preach. If ideas fail to come, pause."[13]

Buckley has laid out the essential steps:

---

[13] Buckley, *Extemporaneous Oratory*, 420–21.

1. Select a theme with which you're familiar, one that stirs your own heart and has had intimate relations with your deepest experiences.
2. Meditate upon it.
3. Take a large view and mark out some grand divisions (ignore details, think only of what will illustrate your thought—not with the purpose of using any particular illustration, but of filling your mind with appropriate similitudes).
4. Then preach.

These basic steps are the essentials of preaching on your feet. You'll notice that they follow the "unplanned structure" form above. It's my conviction that this is the highest and most satisfying form of preaching on your feet. It is also the form that gives the greatest freedom to your unique personality, your growing skill, and the leading of the Spirit. In my own experience I use all of the methods mentioned in this chapter, but it comes down to three basic phases:

1. Study the passage or topic thoroughly.
2. Strategize your approach.
3. Set your heart and mind to preach.

The first two steps have largely been covered here, but the third step, that of setting the "heart and mind," is the most individual of all. It is important in preaching the Word of God to have thoroughly studied and to have some confidence about how you intend to approach the topic (even if it includes only the final point you wish to make). Setting the heart and mind through prayer and reflection, through quietness, through listening to the congregation sing before you rise to preach; whatever means you employ, it is important to make sure that your spirit is set properly for the moment of preaching. The most important thing for me to do is to draw myself inward to where I am, as best I can, fully aware of the presence of the Lord Jesus in my heart, and remember His call for me to stand before the people and give the message He has laid out before me. As an individual, you will be well served to sort out the best way for you to prepare your heart and mind to preach.

Final Thoughts

I have three important final things to note in the process of preparation.

1. Think on Paper

Even though you are taking no paper or notes into the pulpit, thinking on paper is incredibly important. A landmark study displayed that geniuses of the modern era tend to do something most "average" people do not do, and that is to make abundant private notes as they think.[14] There's something in the feedback loop with the human mind and heart such that seeing what you're saying, playing with words, working with how they're framed—all help create a further and complete understanding. This is directly related to the Socratic method, which appreciates how the interaction with the student causes the tutor himself to learn all the more. It also underscores the importance of talking the

---

[14] Researcher Catherine Cox studied biographies of 300 geniuses from history during the 1920s. Her survey revealed patterns of habits and personality traits among the geniuses, including "compulsive scribbling." Cox noted that each genius had "a penchant for eloquently recording thoughts and feelings in diaries, poems, and letters to friends and family, starting from an early age." Win Wenger and Richard Poe, *The Einstein Factor: A Proven New Method for Increasing Your Intelligence* (Rocklin, CA: Prima, 1996), 59.

passage through. Both in words spoken and words written, the opportunity to make connections and clarify understanding is immeasurable. Webb stresses the same point:

> Whatever the processes, however, if one is planning a sermon to be preached without notes, one thing becomes paramount: you take detailed notes on your examination of the text. You can say, "Of course I take notes when I do my exegetical work," but the point is that when you work on or think through a text that will be part of a sermon preached without notes, it is even more important that your findings and thoughts be carefully and meticulously recorded. This, in fact, is the first key difference in how one prepares to preach without manuscript or notes.[15]

These notes give an additional opportunity for you to return to the passage and the sermon someday, not repeating the exact one but in a fresh way being able to work through your previous thoughts and adding new ones as you bring a fresh meal to a hopeful audience.

2. Don't Overprepare

One of the strange dangers of preaching on your feet is the actual possibility of overpreparing—gathering so much information, so many thoughts, so much detail that you as a preacher are overwhelmed and your temptation will be to ramble and overwhelm your audience as well. Richard S. Storrs told Buckley that he at first failed in extemporizing because he had overprepared. "He had written out heads,

---

[15] Webb, *Preaching without Notes*, 38.

subdivisions, even some passages or paragraphs in full, that he might be certain to have material enough."[16] Much of our study must be buried so that we give our listeners the essential gems we have found and not the bucket of sand drawn out in the process.

3. Watch Your Energy

In my experience it is as important to make sure I'm well rested for preaching. In some ways, given the nature of preparation as an ongoing process, if a choice is needed between more preparation and resting, resting would make the biggest difference. Macartney observes, "When body and mind are tired, it is hard to preach in any fashion, and doubly hard to preach without notes. Therefore the importance of the care of the body. It has been well said that if the preacher does not sleep over his sermon Saturday night, the congregation will sleep over it on Sunday morning."[17]

---

[16] Buckley, *Extemporaneous Oratory*, 417–19.
[17] Clarence Edward Macartney, *Preaching without Notes* (Grand Rapids: Baker, 1946), 155–56.

Chapter 10

Delivery on Your Feet

t the outset I must confess that the study of delivery is absurd. The volumes on delivery are almost limitless and usually have as their main concern an attempt to teach the speaker how to sound better than he really does. Broadus underscored the foolishness of this notion by asserting:

> The idea of becoming eloquent merely by the study of structure, of voice, and of gesture is essentially absurd. Delivery does not consist merely, or even chiefly, in vocalization and gesticulation, but it implies that one is possessed with the subject, that he is completely in sympathy with it and fully alive to its importance, that he is not repeating remembered words but setting free the thoughts shut up in his mind.[1]

Many years ago Andy Wileman, who was at that time the assistant to John Walvoord, president of Dallas Theological

---

[1] John A. Broadus and Vernon L. Stanfield, *On the Preparation and Delivery of Sermons*, 4th ed. (San Francisco: Harper & Row, 1979), 264.

Seminary, shared with me over coffee the final result from the leadership center of a major university "back east." "What they discovered about leadership," Andy said, "is that leadership cannot be taught, but it can be learned." In other words, something as individualized as leadership is not the sort of thing that can simply be taught to anyone. But if an individual has an aptitude, then of course that person can learn leadership by good instruction and his or her own individual efforts. Concerning delivery on your feet, the same principle applies. Delivery cannot be taught, but it can be learned. Let's consider a few strategic insights in order to get on the path of learning.

Delivery Is Connected to Preparation

Since preaching on your feet requires the saturation of the speaker for the outpouring of all that he's learned, preparation and delivery are intimately related. Broadus adds, "Whatever be the method of preparing, what has been done should be regarded as but preparation; the sermon must be cherished and kept alive in the mind, must be vitally a part of itself, and then as living, breathing thought it will be delivered."[2] The living nature of a sermon or a message gives rise to the appropriate kind of delivery. Delivery, if it is to be anything, is to be personal and natural.

Delivery Is Personal

Throughout this book we have talked about the importance of individuality and the preacher's personality. Delivery is the place at which this key ingredient glares to the preacher

---

[2] Ibid.

and the audience. Again Broadus gives us the summary, "It should be the spontaneous product of the speaker's particular personality, as acted on by the subject which now fills his mind and heart."[3] Preaching on your feet is about the spontaneous product of true preparation. Delivery occurs in the moment.

The fact for the preacher to accept is that his personality is engaged through the power of feeling or burden for his subject. Harvard professor Henry Ware Jr. underscored this point in 1831:

> Cicero tells us of himself, that the instances in which he was most successful, were those in which he most entirely abandoned himself to the impulses of feeling. Every speaker's experience will bear testimony to the same thing; and thus the saying of Goldsmith proves true, that "to feel one's subject thoroughly, and to speak without fear, are the only rules of eloquence." Let him who would preach successfully, remember this, in the choice of subjects for extemporaneous efforts, let him have regard to it, and never encumber himself nor distress his hearers, with the attempt to interest them in a subject, which excites at the moment only a feeble interest in his own mind.[4]

Of course it is not always possible to abandon oneself utterly to the impulse of feeling. But Cicero's point, as many preachers throughout history also confirm, is that the possession of the message by the speaker is the exact thing that engages

---

[3] Ibid.

[4] Henry Ware Jr., *Hints on Extemporaneous Preaching* (Boston: Hilliard, Gray, Little and Wilkins, 1831), 88, http://www.prism.net/user/fcarpenter/warejr.html (accessed July 13, 2007).

the true personality. The sermon from start to finish is to be uniquely your own; therefore, in preparation, in structuring, and in delivery, nothing in it should particularly remind any listener of any other speaker he or she has ever heard.

Delivery Is Natural

Charles Haddon Spurgeon, undoubtedly one of the greatest preachers in history, was known for his natural delivery. Revisit Dallimore's comment: "In his delivery Spurgeon was entirely natural. There was nothing 'put on' about him, and although a note of humor often crept into what he was saying, the whole of his preaching was overshadowed by his tremendous earnestness."[5] Even in this example we can see the connection between earnestness or feeling and Spurgeon's natural (and not "put on") delivery style. Even so, a great host of preachers arose to copy or sound like Spurgeon. Spurgeon alone sounded like Spurgeon. As soon as imitation of delivery is engaged, the uniqueness of the person and the naturalness of delivery is gone.

Clyde Reid brings us this insight from Helmut Thielicke:

> The way the minister talks about religion is one symptom of this integrity crisis. If the preacher talks about modern art and drama naturally, but speaks of religion in a special tone of voice as though it were something from another world, he reveals his separation of religion and life. He does

---

[5] Arnold A. Dallimore, *Spurgeon* (Chicago: Moody, 1984), 84.

not really do his thinking, feeling, and willing in
the same world as his world of faith.[6]

Thielicke's point or concern is that the life of faith of the
minister is not connected to the actual life he lives. This is
the exact problem in the pulpit. When a preacher is a different person in the pulpit than he is in his day-to-day life, all
integrity is gone. It is natural to become more animated and
a little more exaggerated in public communication; but the
seed of that communication must be in the day-to-day life of
the person, or it comes across as nothing but fakery. Fakery
itself can be popular, but popularity is rarely a mechanism
of change in the people but rather a reflection of what the
people want. In Paul's words to Timothy, fakery for the sake
of winning the crowd is soothing "itching ears" (2 Tim 4:3).

Ken Howard, an actor of some renown in our day, has
written a book on acting and speaking called *Act Natural*.
Howard argues that acting involves the bringing of the personality into the character that is being played rather than
the common way we think; an actor must take on a different personality. A number of Howard's points bear repeating. Howard observes that we all play out a variety of roles
throughout our day: "The pitch you make to the bank man-
ager for a loan is bound to be different from your toast at
your best friend's wedding."[7] In either situation we may be
more animated or more logical, but it is still our unique personality that comes to bear on that situation. He exhorts, if

---

[6] Clyde Reid, *The Empty Pulpit: A Study in Preaching as Communication*
(New York: Harper & Row, 1967), 43–44, referring to Helmut Thielicke, *The
Trouble with the Church*, trans. John W. Doberstein (New York: Harper & Row,
1965).

[7] Ken Howard, *Act Natural: How to Speak to Any Audience* (New York:
Random House, 2003), 54.

not begs, the speaker never to write a speech: "You'll never be able to convey any sense of reality by reading a speech. Even if you are blessed with a natural photographic memory, do not write your speech and memorize it verbatim. That, too, is likely to undermine your effort to seem spontaneous and real."[8]

Here again, in the most recent of books, the historic fact is offered that audiences want authenticity. I'm personally convinced that if you see a person who sounds fake as a speaker, he comes from a tradition where there was one originator who spoke in that manner, and it sounded authentic from that particular individual. Unfortunately, the more we copy one another's speeches, and the more we attempt to read or memorize these speeches, the more our own personality and naturalness leaks away, which can only mean we grasp at some mask to wear in hope of keeping the audience on our side.

After explaining the importance of understanding that "acting is what you do" (by this he means that acting is about the actions you take, and no matter, public speaking or public theater, actions are included in the communication), he connects naturalness to language by telling us:

> Your presentation will be in your language, in the order you have chosen, with anecdotes that are a part of your life, using your own physicality. Remember the time when your father opened up the hood and got splattered with oil? All of a sudden, a demonstration on how to fix an auto-

---

[8] Ibid., 55.

mobile engine becomes a funny story from your own life.[9]

Here is the essence of naturalness, that is, your own language, your own experiences, recaptured and offered to a specific audience. Howard also gives us further good advice in the process of delivery in order to stay natural: "At any point in your remarks, you should be able to answer the question, 'How does what I'm doing serve my objective?'"[10] He's reminding us that having a main point, an objective with our message, is strategic because it then allows (in our own natural language) a spontaneous birth of words, action, inflection, and expression that fully communicate your earnestness for the message.

> I recognized Olympia's (Dukakis) choices as a classic example of Stella Adler's constant exhortation to students, "Make it your own!"—another acting technique that is indispensable to public speakers. You are, after all, playing yourself. Ironically, when most people perform in public, they fail to get themselves right. ("He is so much better in private," your friends assure the other members of your audience.)[11]

"Playing yourself" is still in large measure an act, but it is an authentic one that engages the whole person. If you're animated and effective in communication in your living room, then bringing that into the pulpit will change everything. Howard clarifies this point with the following:

---

[9] Ibid., 76.
[10] Ibid., 77.
[11] Ibid., 66–67.

Acting is bringing as much of yourself to the character as possible to make the role come alive on stage. You must personalize everything you can. . . .

In working with young actors I have found that they will improve very quickly once they understand the difference between turning the character into themselves and bringing parts of themselves into the role in order to connect to the character more personally. The character is yours and will be revealed by your way of playing his actions, rather than how someone else might do it.[12]

The Three Ps

Some years ago I spoke at a Junior League meeting in which I was able to share the gospel two times without offending a single soul (I was just using the first P). I spoke on how to speak in public. I offered three words that begin with *P* to explain the essentials of public speaking. These principles have served many well. In fact, my favorite comment was from a woman who stopped me at the local mall, recognized who I was, and mentioned that after my talk, she was able to speak publicly for the first time in her life after years and years of hoping somehow to overcome her fear. The three Ps are largely review, so consider them as such.

Passion (P¹)

By passion I mean that you must have something you really care about in your talk. This whole book has been about the importance of caring for the message, of having

[12] Ibid., 70.

"a warm heart," as Whitefield said. I shared with the Junior League ladies that I didn't particularly get excited about teaching people about public speaking, but I did particularly get excited about sharing my faith in Christ. In other words, I was explaining the passion point and giving the illustration of something I was personally passionate about. In particular, I am burdened for how people turn Christianity into a set of external rules to control behavior, when the Bible clearly teaches that the transformation is from the inside out (see Gal 2:20; Rom 7:4–6). The point is if you are not passionate about the passage you happen to be on, include something in the message related to the passage that you actually can be passionate about. If, indeed, you're not passionate at all, you're best to follow Rick Warren's advice mentioned earlier, "If I don't feel it, I forget it."

Personality (P²)

Not only do you need passion, but you also need to speak through your personality, your voice, your style, your language. Of course, this has been our conversation in the delivery section and throughout much of the book so there's no need to belabor the point.

Practice (P³)

Practice occurs in two ways: (1) practicing a specific talk, and (2) practicing speaking in general. In order to learn to preach, you must simply preach.

In learning how to preach on your feet, more opportunities create the confidence and the skill; but, when you are alone, you can actually practice preaching extemporaneously. One of the most powerful things you can do is to pretend you have an audience before you and talk through the passage aloud. This process of hearing yourself speak, watching words come to mind, and clarifying points on the spot will demonstrate to you this capacity that God has given you to use. Practicing an extemporaneous sermon is an excellent way to prepare an extemporaneous sermon. Most of us actually understand this if we ever tell jokes or stories. The first, second, or third time we tell a joke it's not as good because we haven't yet settled in our mind the story, the sequence, and the timing. But after telling it a few times, it becomes natural. Much of the learning and studying in communication that all of us do is built on prior experiences with communication; the more you practice preaching on your feet, the better you're going to be. I do want to warn you, however, not to dabble with this. Give it a real try; as Buckley observed, in about six weeks you'll be well on your way to effectively learning how to preach on your feet. Six weeks, of course, is just a start; six years will begin to get you closer to mastery.

Conclusion

The key to delivery is not technique, but heart. In 1831 Henry Ware identified "a devoted heart" as "the great essential requisite to effective preaching." He concluded:

> After all, therefore, which can be said, the great essential requisite to effective preaching in this method (or indeed in any method) is a devoted heart. A strong religious sentiment, leading to a fervent zeal for the good of other men, is better than all rules of art; it will give him courage,

which no science or practice could impart, and open his lips boldly, when the fear of man would keep them closed. . . . Art may fail him, and all his treasures of knowledge desert him; but if his heart be warm with love, he will "speak right on," aiming at the heart, and reaching the heart, and satisfied to accomplish the great purpose, whether he be thought to do it tastefully or not.[13]

[13] Ware, *Hints on Extemporaneous Preaching*, 94.

Chapter 11

Spirit-Led on Your Feet

*N*o preacher, teacher, or student worth his
salt would deny the importance of the
Holy Spirit's role in communicating God's
Word. The problem, however, arises with our tendency to
think in black-and-white ways. Something is "of God," "not
of God," "in the Spirit," "in the flesh," "written," or "spontaneous," and the like. These are the order of the day. When
we think biblically and practically, however, these distinc-
tions are not always so airtight as hoped. Ramesh Richard
exemplifies this tendency as it relates to the spiritual in
preaching:

> Those who consistently preach extemporane-
> ously may succumb to any momentary inspiration
> (often under the guise of spontaneity), lack vari-
> ety in style, and repeat similar themes and illustra-
> tions because they have not prepared or planned
> their sermons. Except in the most unusual of cir-
> cumstances, please do not attempt extemporane-

ous preaching if you want to feed your people a good, steady diet of God's Word.[1]

Richard seems to hearken back to Karl Barth's assertion that "only a sermon in which every word can be justified may be said to be a sacramental action." In the same passage Barth, in summary, believes that any discourse other than written should not be considered a Christian discourse at all.[2]

In fairness, however, Richard's concerns are understandable. He wants thoughtful preaching with variety and style that feeds people on a steady diet of God's Word. Nothing about manuscripting a sermon guarantees avoiding any of these maladies in preaching. Fears about preaching are easy to imagine. Consider Richard's worries reframed from the other extreme:

> Those who consistently preach by manuscripting may succumb to a stale inspiration (often under the guise of being well thought out), lack variety and style because it always sounds written, and not repeat similar themes and illustrations often enough to be learned because they have over prepared and over controlled their sermon planning. Except in the most unusual circumstances, please do not attempt manuscript preaching if you want to feed your people a good, heartfelt, and steady diet of God's Word.

---

[1] Ramesh Richard, *Preparing Expository Sermons: A Seven-Step Method for Biblical Preaching* (Grand Rapids: Baker, 1995), 131.

[2] Karl Barth, *The Preaching of the Gospel*, trans. B. E. Hooke (Philadelphia: Westminster Press, 1963), 77–78.

Obviously a preacher may not feed his people a good diet from God's Word, whether he plans excessively or preaches extemporaneously. Dr. Richard probably understands the word *extemporaneous* to refer to impromptu speaking rather than preaching on your feet as a result of hard work. Specifically there is nothing in true extemporaneous preaching that means a sermon is unprepared or unplanned. Indeed, as one matures in the faith the ability to speak in an "unplanned way" largely disappears.

> One day in the House of Commons, British Prime Minister Disraeli made a brilliant speech on the spur of the moment. That night a friend said to him, "I must tell you how much I enjoyed your extemporaneous talk. It's been on my mind all day." "Madam," confessed Disraeli, "that extemporaneous talk has been on my mind for twenty years!"[3]

The heart of the issue with overpreparation, manuscripting, or thick outlines is found in Dr. Richard's statement, "may succumb to any momentary inspiration (often under the guise of spontaneity)," where this is considered an evil by those who promote manuscripting, but is seen as a noble moment in the leading of the Spirit by those who preach on their feet. Is there a risk of an inappropriate and casual word under a moment of inspiration? Certainly. Is the risk worth it? Absolutely. The ability to listen to God and pay attention to the response of the audience allows the person who has grown in his ability to preach on his feet to listen to the

---

[3] Miles J. Stanford, *The Complete Green Letters* (Grand Rapids: Zondervan, 1983), 9.

leading of God and make adjustments. The one anchored by his manuscript, noticing a mistake, will muddle through hoping to fix the manuscript for the next time he uses it.

The Fear

This issue concerns the Holy Spirit and control. The leading of the Spirit always occurs in a moment. Whether that moment is at one's desk on Thursday with hopes that the Spirit is leading accurately for Sunday or the Spirit leads in the moment before the people after thorough preparation and reflection, the preacher must be concerned with the spiritual leading at a moment in time. The preacher who depends on manuscripts and thick outlines is invariably hoping to control the information so as not to embarrass himself or do damage to the people. The fact remains, however, that manuscripting does not take away the possibility of embarrassment or damage. It only gives the preacher a sense of control, much as holding a steering wheel gives comfort to the one going over a cliff in a speeding vehicle. The real to key to overcoming all the fears in preaching is to walk in the Spirit in both preparation and delivery, "For God hath not given us a spirit of fear; but of power, and of love, and of a sound mind" (2 Tim 1:7 KJV).

The Nature of the Spirit

The Spirit of God, for all our debate and discussion, still remains largely a mystery. Christ's words probably give more insight by inviting us to pull up short in our understanding than any of the words of Scripture. "The wind blows where it wishes, and you hear the sound of it, but cannot tell where it comes from and where it goes. So is everyone who is born of the Spirit" (John 3:8). After I came to faith in my college years, I realized that it wasn't so much the gospel I had missed in my college years; it was the Holy Spirit Himself. I believed the gospel when I heard it because I had been readied by God; but the role of the Holy Spirit was both intriguing and confusing. In my denominational upbringing the Spirit of God was hardly mentioned. And yet, as I began to understand that God had given us His very Spirit to empower the Christian's life and walk before Him, nothing was ever the same for me.

The nature of the Spirit is easy enough to understand since He is the third person of the Trinity. The Spirit of God, as all orthodox Christians believe, is a separate and equal person within the oneness of God. He is referred to in many ways scripturally such as the Spirit of holiness (Rom 1:4), the Spirit of adoption (Rom 8:15), and the Spirit of promise (Eph 1:13). Of all the terms for the Holy Spirit, however, no two affect our preaching like Spirit of grace and Spirit of truth.

In setting forth the new work of God, John wrote, "The Word became flesh and dwelt among us, and we beheld His glory, the glory as of the only begotten of the Father, full of grace and truth" (John 1:14). It is the nature of the Lord's ministry, and furthered through the writing of Paul and the other New Testament authors, that grace and truth take center stage in the life of the believer. John wrote of the coming Spirit, "But when the Helper comes, whom I shall send to you from the Father, the Spirit of truth who proceeds from the Father, He will testify of Me" (John 15:26). And again, "However, when He, the Spirit of truth, has come, He will guide you into all truth; for He will not speak on His own *authority*, but whatever He hears He will speak; and He will tell you things to come" (John 16:13). He is the Spirit of truth. This explains J. Vernon McGee's observation at a graduation ceremony: "The Word of God is the track on which the train of the Holy Spirit rides." The fact that He is the Spirit of truth also explains the parallel in the following two passages:

> And do not be drunk with wine, in which is dissipation; but be filled with the Spirit, speaking to one another in psalms and hymns and spiritual songs, singing and making melody in your heart to the Lord, giving thanks always for all things to God the Father in the name of our Lord Jesus Christ, submitting to one another in the fear of God (Eph 5:18–21).

> Let the word of Christ dwell in you richly in all wisdom, teaching and admonishing one another in psalms and hymns and spiritual songs, singing with grace in your hearts to the Lord (Col 3:16).

These passages show a perfect interchange between the word of Christ and the Spirit of God. In other words, to be word filled is to be Spirit filled, which makes perfect sense if He indeed is the Spirit of truth. If our preaching, be it written or extemporaneous, is not Spirit led, then it is not offering the diet of truth so needed in the life of every Christian (1 Pet 2:2).

The Spirit of God is also called the Spirit of grace (Heb 10:29), and it is indeed grace that must govern our preaching thematically. Many years ago I discovered an old tape of Lewis Sperry Chafer teaching at Dallas Theological Seminary. I was struck by his sincerity as I listened to his reasoned and soft voice. His appeal was made along this line: "Gentlemen," he said "please do not preach against the world. The world and all it offers is the only anesthesia that people have for the pain they experience. The more you preach against it, the more they will cling to their pain reliever. Instead, preach grace and make the appeal to the kindness of God the thing they may grasp when they let go of the world." I am recalling his words as best I can, but they expressed the sentiment and certainly echo Paul's emphasis: "For the grace of God that brings salvation has appeared to all men, teaching us that, denying ungodliness and worldly lusts, we should live soberly, righteously, and godly in the present age" (Titus 2:11–12). A Spirit-led preacher is filled with the Spirit of God and the messages of grace and truth.

The Nature of Leadership

It is common in our thinking to emphasize the role of the Holy Spirit without thinking clearly about what leadership means. Leadership itself has been a subject of great debate and misunderstanding through the ages. The pendulum often swings from being courageous and "out in front of the troops" to being a servant leader and hardly being seen by the troops. Fritz explains leadership in simple terms: "A leader is someone who clearly has a place to go. Most believe he will probably get there, and he invites followers to join with him."[4] The invitation separates leadership from coercion, and of course vision is paramount. When one is leading, he

---

[4] Robert Fritz, *The Path of Least Resistance: Learning to Become the Creative Force in Your Life* (New York: Ballentine, 1989), 140.

is inviting others to pursue a future place and a future result that is better than the current moment. Often many do not follow the leader, but as Christ's example displays, simply "being followed" is not the only proof of leadership.

The Spirit Is Always Leading

Perhaps no passage better combines the nature of the Spirit and the nature of leadership than Gal 5:25: "If we live in the Spirit, let us also walk in the Spirit." The truth is that the Spirit is always leading. There is perhaps no more powerful metaphor than walking in the Spirit. The first illustration of this truth I ever heard was that of a son following his father in the snow. The son was working to make his steps follow exactly those of his father. In Alabama I rarely experienced snow, but I did know what it was like to be bird hunting as a young boy and trying to step widely in a muddy and swampy path to stay in the exact steps of my father, for they were the path of safety.

In preaching the Word of God, the Spirit is always leading. He is leading in our study. He is leading in our writing. He is leading in the preparation of our heart on Sunday morning, and He is leading in the moment of delivery. The fact that He is leading, however, does not guarantee that we are following. Our following comes down to the essential nature of our freedom.

The Nature of Freedom

We Christians often seem to misunderstand the nature of freedom, more than most folks. A common idea is that freedom isn't doing whatever you *want* to do; freedom is doing

what you *ought* to do. But is this really the nature of freedom? Galatians 5:1 says, "Stand fast therefore in the liberty
by which Christ has made us free, and do not be entangled
again with a yoke of bondage." The New American Standard
Bible states, "It was for freedom that Christ set us free; therefore keep standing firm and do not be subject again to a yoke
of slavery." In either case the scriptural claim is that Christ
has given us freedom. Freedom, however, has at its core genuine choice. Jerry Clower, the Southern comedian, describes
how hunters always gave the racoon a sporting chance. If the
racoon can come out of a tree and whip the 20 dogs that are
chasing him, he is free to walk away. This idea of freedom of
choice is not really what Paul has in mind. When there is no
choice, there is no freedom.

Naturally, when we consider the common Christian man-
tra on this point, "Freedom isn't doing whatever you want to
do, freedom is doing what you ought to do," we see that we
have simply placed a new obligation on the believer. The
uncomfortable truth is that freedom means we can choose or
not choose. Indeed, Galatians 5:1 tells us that there is a genuine option for the Christian. He may either walk in freedom
or return to being a slave. This slavery, according to Paul,
is especially a return to the law. The law in Paul's thinking
was more than simply the Old Testament law; instead it dealt
with the legal principle. The legal principle itself is essentially obligation, such that if one obeys the law he is blessed;
if he disobeys the law, he is cursed. The New Testament saint
has an entirely different relationship with the Old Testament
law or any law, as Paul spells out concerning our walk in the
Spirit.

> Therefore, my brethren, you also have become dead to the law through the body of Christ, that you may be married to another—to Him who was raised from the dead, that we should bear fruit to God. For when we were in the flesh, the sinful passions which were aroused by the law were at work in our members to bear fruit to death. But now we have been delivered from the law, having died to what we were held by, so that we should serve in the newness of the Spirit and not *in* the oldness of the letter (Rom 7:4–6).

Obviously the believer can live under the law or live under sin, but Paul certainly does not believe that this is the call of God. God has called us to walk in the Spirit because of the newfound freedom we have in Christ Jesus. The Word of God tells us that human beings, before coming to faith in Christ in any final assessment, are not truly free; that is, they are obligated to follow the dictates of the flesh.

The freedom we have in Christ, which maintains the fact that we can choose to be under the law in sin or under the Spirit of life, affects both our understanding of the audience and our approach to Spirit-led preaching. No matter the techniques, gifting, and talents of the preacher, if his message is devoid of the grace of God and the freedom found in following the Spirit, then what good is it? Additionally, if the preacher is so obligated and bound by his notes and formulas that he cannot listen to the direction of the Spirit in his preaching, then what good is this as well?

Some might consider this too mystical in a walk with God. Admittedly, there is something mysterious about the work of the Spirit of God in the life of believer or the preacher. Mystery itself seems provided for and "boundried" by the Word of God. Philippians 4:6–7 speaks of experiencing peace that is beyond comprehension. First Thessalonians 4:9 states, "But concerning brotherly love you have no need that I should write to you, for you yourselves are taught by God to love one another." Paul seems to understand that God Himself can work in the Spirit, and the spirits of the Thessalonian believers, such that He is said directly to "teach them to love one another." The mysterious aspect of a walk with God in our preaching and in our ministries is risky business. It seems, however, that it is a risky business that God is intent on honoring.

All of this is best understood through the role of faith. We come to God by faith in Jesus Christ, and we walk with God by faith in Jesus Christ. In the clearest and simplest of ways, this explains why in this fresh age of the church we are not under law. Galatians 3:12 states this simply: "Yet the law is not of faith." When one walks under law, one is walking by sight. And though many will aim charges[5] at the elect of God for daring to walk by faith and not by sight (2 Cor 5:7), the words of Douglas Moo answer the concerns clearly:

> An approach that eliminates the Mosaic Law as binding authority for Christians is sometimes accused of being "antinomian" and opening the door to ethical relativity. But two replies to this accusation must be made. First, the position

---

[5] Usually the pejorative term "antinomian" is applied to those of us who assert we are under grace, not under law. This old term has a long and sordid history starting with the Catholic accusation of Reformers as antinomian, on to the Puritan attacks against proponents of grace, and even to our present day among various writers and theologians.

outlined here holds that Christians are not under the *Mosaic* Law, not that they are free from *all* law. The distinction between the Mosaic Law, which is clearly what the NT writers mean 95 percent of the time when they use the word "law," and the theological concept of "law" needs to be carefully observed. We have seen that the distinction has its roots in the NT, where Paul can distinguish between the Law of Moses and the Law of God (1 Cor 9:20–21). Failure to observe this distinction has resulted in considerable confusion and misunderstanding. Second, in the fear about ethical nihilism, one senses a failure to appreciate the power of God's Spirit operative in the believer. When the "antinomian" implications of Paul's teaching were raised as an objection against that teaching, Paul responded not by introducing a "new law" but by pointing to the Spirit (Gal 5:16ff.) and to union with Christ (Rom 6). To be sure, there needs to be recognition of the fact that Christians often fail to walk in accordance with that Spirit and need "law" to correct and discipline them (Luther is eloquent on this point). But any approach that substitutes external commands for the Spirit as the basic norm for Christian living runs into serious difficulties with Paul.[6]

---

[6] Douglas J. Moo, "The Law of Moses or the Law of Christ," in *Continuity and Discontinuity: Perspectives on the Relationship Between the Old and New Testaments*, ed. John S. Feinberg (Westchester, IL: Crossway, 1988), 218.

The Nature of Relationship

The nature of relationship is the best explanation of a walk with the ever-leading Spirit. Each relationship is a unique combination of two individuals who essentially say yes to having a relationship. In the math of relationships, it only takes one to say no for there to be no relationship. In the preacher's relationship with God, God has said yes and the preacher has said yes. The final result is that something that has never before existed now exits, that is, the relationship between you and your God. On the human level we can see that the uniqueness of two individuals in combination makes for a completely unique interaction. Why would this not be true in your own relationship with God? One of the great difficulties in following the Spirit is learning to unhand formulas and to embrace a unique and individual walk with the One who formed us. This is the flavor of the unique white stone mentioned in Rev 2:17; only the individual and God know the name written on it. To preach on your feet you must learn to be true to yourself before the Lord in a unique and living relationship with Him.

The Answer

The answer to the Spirit-led life of preaching on your feet is found in the simple relationship between three verses for your reflection.

And *whatever* you do in word or deed, *do* all
in the name of the Lord Jesus, giving thanks to
God the Father through Him (Col 3:17).

As each one has received a gift, minister it
to one another, as good stewards of the manifold
grace of God. If anyone speaks, *let him speak* as
the oracles of God. If anyone ministers, *let him
do it* as with the ability which God supplies, that
in all things God may be glorified through Jesus
Christ, to whom belong the glory and the domin-
ion forever and ever. Amen (1 Pet 4:10–11).

But without faith *it is* impossible to please
Him, for he who comes to God must believe that
He is, and *that* He is a rewarder of those who dili-
gently seek Him (Heb 11:6).

Again, this is a by-faith proposition, that is to say, preaching on your feet is about an intimate and in-the-moment
walk with God. If you preach unto Him and speak in faith
as an oracle of God, then how will the Lord respond except
to reward you? Using a written manuscript or thick outline
is no more a guarantee to make a sermon sacred than aris-
ing noteless in the moment before an audience after careful
study and reflection. The guarantee comes to the preacher
who walks in faith before his Lord.

Chapter 12

Expository Preaching on Your Feet

dvocates of expository preaching have always been the most highly resistant opponents of preaching on your feet. The objection is so important that it demands a short discussion with the hope of convincing those committed to expository preaching that it is perhaps the best suited of all sermon types to preaching on your feet. I consider myself an expository preacher, almost exclusively, and have experienced no greater joy in study and in preaching than expository preaching through an extemporaneous delivery.

Expository Preaching Misdefined

Expository preaching is popularly misdefined as preaching that explains the Bible book by book and line by line. You will hardly find this definition in any authoritative resource, but those who most care for expository preaching at the grassroots level misunderstand it in this way. Often their experience in reading or in their personal church history has at its core individuals who taught book by book and verse by verse. In the past one hundred years, preachers like Martin Lloyd-Jones, John McArthur, Ray Stedman, and J. Vernon McGee quickly come to mind.

Its Value

The value of understanding exposition as book-by-book and line-by-line preaching is that it encourages a meatier explanation of the Word of God. Surely many of the problems we face in our current experience of Christianity involve rather shallow and on-the-low-shelf preaching. Of course reaching out to the lost requires offering them the milk of the Word, but many preachers never get beyond the milk. As a result a great deal of the immaturity and shallowness in American Christianity can be blamed on the pulpit. Additionally, no matter how a church tries to supplement its teaching with more advanced studies in small groups and Sunday schools, the pulpit perpetually sets the tone for the church.

Those who equate expository preaching with verse-by-verse and line-by-line preaching tend to develop much smaller churches that confuse spiritual vibrancy with more knowledge. Earl Radmacher has correctly observed, "I cannot receive what I do not believe, and I cannot believe what I do not know. Therefore, it begins with knowledge." This is true, but unfortunately many churches and expositors who obsess on book-by-book and line-by-line preaching simply cultivate a following of individuals who often replace living the Word with knowing the Word. No doubt there are exceptions, but when they are studied carefully, they turn out to be just that—exceptions.

Its Weakness

The weakness with the definition of expository preaching as book by book and line by line is threefold. First, there is no example of this kind of expository preaching in the Bible. This may surprise some, but nowhere does the Bible give examples of any individuals ever being in the midst of a study of an entire book of the Bible given book by book and line by line to the people. It certainly makes sense to study and explain passages in this way since this is exactly how we understand any piece of literature, especially a letter. No one, however, can demonstrate conclusively that book by book and line by line was ever the New Testament or Old Testament directive from God through His Word.

Second, this misdefinition of expository preaching leads to preaching series that are simply too long. In my first experience as a preacher, I took two years to teach the book of Ephesians. I also took two years to preach through the book of Galatians, and one year (I was blazing along) to teach through the book of James. That is simply too long for a practical reason: newcomers and visitors inevitably feel like they are in the middle of a conversation and will tend to consider coming back when the preacher begins a new, lengthy series.

Third, this misdefinition of expository preaching often loses the point of the book. The scholar who works diligently to explain every detail of a text eventually loses connection with the overall picture. Of course, a preacher can return to reemphasize the point of the book, but that makes the study even longer.

Finally, this type of preaching often results when the preacher attempts to follow what has been modeled by a professor. If all church members were as motivated as seminary students, who are called and who pay for their education, then the book-by-book and line-by-line approach would make a world of sense. But the preacher's congregation is made up of a great mixture of individuals who are at various stages of growth and maturity. Much as a parent must consider appropriate diet given the age of a child, the preacher must give an appropriate diet of the Word of God considering the people he seeks to serve.

Its True Definition

True expository preaching is always about the passage and its structure, no matter the topic or approach in preaching. According to Merrill Unger,

> if a clear and unconfused definition is to be arrived at, the valid criterion, it would seem, is not the length of the portion treated, whether a single verse or a larger unit, but the manner of treatment. No matter what the length of the portion explained may be, if it is handled in such a way that its real and essential meaning as it existed in the mind of the particular Bible writer and as it exists in the light of the overall context of Scripture is made plain and applied to present-day needs of the hearers, it may properly be said to be expository preaching.[1]

---

[1] Merrill F. Unger, *Principles of Expository Preaching* (Grand Rapids: Zondervan, 1955), 33.

Haddon Robinson defines expository preaching as "the communication of a biblical concept, derived from and transmitted through a historical, grammatical, and literary study of a passage in its context, which the Holy Spirit first applies to the personality and experience of the preacher, then through him to his hearers."[2] Unger and Robinson hit at the essential point, which is that the truth being taught is derived from the passage and not forced on the passage. Moreover, they insist that in an expository sermon a text is explained, understood, and applied to the listener. All preaching should really be expository preaching according to this definition. In other words, whether someone is explaining the gospel, considering a topic, or teaching a book of the Bible, the truth being explored should be derived from at least one text of Scripture.

Expository Preaching on Your Feet

If expository preaching is fundamentally biblical preaching rather than mere human reasoning or entertaining talk, and if expository preaching comes from the text and is not imposed upon the text, then expository preaching is the approach best suited for preaching on your feet.

Why is expository preaching the easiest type of preaching to pursue extemporaneously? The reason is simple: the text is the outline! Because the aim is to saturate oneself with the Word of God and to understand the passage so clearly that it can be taught without notes, it only stands to reason that the structure of the passage should give rise to the structure of the sermon. As a preacher develops his skill, he

---

[2] Haddon W. Robinson, *Biblical Preaching: The Development of Expository Messages* (Grand Rapids: Baker, 1980), 20.

will be ready at any moment with passages he has studied intensely to open the Word of God, to see the outline within the text, and to preach from his heart in a new moment for a new audience. Of course there may be an infinite number of ways to structure a presentation for an audience; the text itself almost dictates its own outline. Even though templates may be valuable and appropriate, the most powerful way to preach is with a structure the passage offers rather than one which the preacher imposes. This approach helps the listeners because as they read again on Monday the passage preached on Sunday, the same outline will arise in their own thinking and reflection.

Each passage or each book will have its own structure, but it is a mistake to believe that there is simply one structure per passage. Just as the angle at which one looks at a piece of sculpture "changes" the sculpture somewhat, so the flavor of the passage is changed by the angle of approach the preacher takes. This fact is not to say that the meaning of the text changes because the meaning of the text can never change. We know that God did not stutter and that He intended to communicate a specific truth or set of truths through the words He gave us. How that truth is emphasized in the text can vary. Three specific ways to understand the structure of a passage for preaching purposes may be of some help. The three common structural approaches to any passage are the sequential, the logical, and the thematic.

A *sequential outline* considers the flow or the sequence of steps within the passage. This is the most common way to understand an expository outline. First . . ., next . . ., then . . . passages often naturally flow in this manner. Sometimes for effective preaching it is best to start with the conclusion, then to show how the writer reached that conclusion by visiting points one, two, three, and so forth. Either way the structure is essentially sequential. Paul's exploits in the book of Acts are easily appreciated as sequential: many times Paul preaches in a city . . . , is at first accepted . . . , then the crowd turns . . . ; he is tortured/escapes . . . and moves on to the next opportunity in the next town.

The *logical outline* is similar to the sequential, but it looks at the reasoning behind the passage rather than the story line of the passage. This is the logic of practical reasoning (that is, "it makes sense") but is not necessarily formal logic. Commonly a passage can be understood in an "if this, then that" format. John 3:16 can naturally fit this form: If you believe in the Son, then you will have eternal life.

The *thematic outline* generally looks at key words within a passage or any larger section of Scripture. The book of Titus is an excellent example for taking a theme such as "good works" and showing how Paul developed the importance of believers being zealous in the outworking of their faith as essential to a high-impact Christian community and witness.

Nothing inherent in expository preaching demands that an individual make notes to hold on to information. Once the truth is accepted, careful study and reflection can give rise to an understanding of every passage in a structural way; the structure of the studied passage can imbed the outline in such a way that a preacher who has truly reflected on God's truth can arise to open that passage again and again with great consistency and adaptability to the need of the moment as the Spirit leads.

Chapter 13

Frequently Asked Questions about Preaching on Your Feet

he following questions are by and large from other vocational preachers at my request. These individuals, without reading the manuscript, offered a variety of common questions that are frequently asked when a basic definition of preaching on your feet is given. All of these questions are answered throughout this book in detail. This section, however, offers a brief summary and the tying up of a few loose ends.

Question 1: Why don't more people use this method?

The short answer is, who knows? It probably has to do with education and insecurity. Concerning education, in the foreword I quote Karl Barth, who insisted that deviating even one word from a written and prepared manuscript was an act of rank sin. Our systems of higher education are additionally not teaching students how to think on their feet, and most students want to emulate their professors. Professors are speaking to motivated students and have clarity as their primary focus. Clarity and precision come with thorough outlines. Clarity and precision are clearly achieved most effectively through detailed notes. Of course, the flaw here is that the pulpit, though a classroom, is not a seminary classroom.

Insecurity about preaching on your feet comes from a number of sources but largely because the preacher has never tried it. Emerson observed, "The greater part of courage is having done it before." Simply put, preaching on your feet comes with age and maturity and work. At issue is a decision to learn how. Perhaps additionally, seminaries and Bible colleges will begin to reintroduce this approach as a viable method for effectively preaching the Word of God.

Question 2: Is it wrong to use notes or a manuscript?

It could be wrong, but only as it relates to what the Lord has directed the individual preacher to do. Romans 14:23 states, "Whatever *is* not from faith is sin." Preaching is an act of faith. Whether you are trusting the Lord through notes or manuscript, or through your preparation toward an extemporaneous conversation with the audience, it is wrong not to do what God has asked you to do. On the other hand, it would be better to understand the relationship between manuscripts and notes in terms of "good, better, and best." Is it good to preach the Word of God and be faithful to the text, even if you use a manuscript or a thick outline? Absolutely! Is it better to preach on your feet? Absolutely—at least, that is my hope with this book . . . to return us to a standard found biblically and historically in the vast majority of great preachers!

Question 3: What do you do when you misquote, misspeak, or forget a detail?

First, it is noteworthy that this happens less often than you might imagine. If you prepare faithfully, there is surprisingly little misspeaking while preaching. Misquoting normally happens in the same way that misspelling does— you are guessing. If you don't know something for sure, you shouldn't be saying it in a private conversation much less from the pulpit. Misspeaking or slipping on details is handled in much the same way as in a regular conversation over lunch. We say things like, "Let me restate that," or "Excuse me, I misspoke." Audiences certainly understand that. What integrity to catch yourself and clarify it before the listeners. In fact, it offers a great example: giving people the freedom to go ahead and speak without perfection because they have the opportunity to correct statements as they communicate.

Question 4: Are you more likely to say something foolish without notes?

Yes. You are more likely to do so. In my experience, however, you are also more likely to say something incredibly noteworthy in the inspiration of the moment. In many ways preaching on your feet is about a decision between control and impact. With practice there are fewer mistakes, and often the "foolish thing" turns out to add to the ethos or credibility of the speaker. The people suddenly realize that they are talking to someone who is also human and real, which goes a long way in authentically connecting with an audience.

Question 5: Is preaching to the heart more important than preaching to the head?

I'm a firm believer that the Bible approaches the heart in a broader sense than we commonly do. In other words, to refer to the "heart" biblically is usually to refer to the whole person as well as to his inner essence. A unique spirit-to-spirit connection aside, all preaching to the heart must go through the head. To preach to the heart means to connect and preach to the essence of what is involved with choice and decision and motivation. If someone walks out after hearing a message and can't remember a single point, then what good does it do for long-term motivation? Obviously the head, or understanding, is vitally important for preaching.

Question 6: How do you keep yourself from preaching many main points and not just one main point?

Most of this is covered in the book in terms of strategies, tactics, and templates. By way of a short answer, however, preaching on your feet does not mean you have no strategy or plan but rather that your plan is simple enough to understand and remember and explain, much as you would over coffee. This simplicity allows for abundant complexity under each point without worrying about the overall pattern of the message. As discussed earlier, the most powerful outline is one that is derived from the passage the preacher is explaining. In this way the outline is always ready because it's there in the text.

Question 7: What written notes do you leave behind in your office?

This will turn out to be an entirely personal question. Some may prefer to write out sections of their message. In my early experience I found practicing aloud to a pretend audience to be the most helpful way to develop phrasings as well as to play with inflection and gestures. Today most of my notes are doodles where I, on several pages, gather random thoughts and insights. I normally have one page with a passage where I've gone through, after much study, and written out an illustration or two for each line or point in the message. This is more of a brainstorming process than a commitment to the illustration process. Finally, I normally write a basic outline or strategy of how I'm going to approach the passage. All of that is left in the office, as well as the conviction that I must use any of it (though I normally do)!

Question 8: Is it harder to have sermon notes in the bulletin for people to follow you and take notes?

Probably so. I concluded many years ago that my goal is not to get through a book of the Bible but to get a book of the Bible through the people—not to get through the truth of God but to get the truth of God through the people. A simple outline that gives them room to fill in is excellent. Thorough notes will turn out to be no different from taking the notes into the pulpit. Wherever I speak, I instruct people to take whatever notes they care to, in whatever fashion they want. More specifically, I suggest a different method of note taking. I recommend that people write down one, two, or three things that really strike them for their own lives. The next goal is to take those few notes with them throughout the week and reflect on those one, two, or three poignant insights. Down through the years I have come to believe that a person who will take one truth in the Word and truly make it a part of his life on a yearly basis will be ahead of almost everyone else in just a few years. In other words, I remain a skeptic about intensive notes. It largely comes from a classroom model and always has as its aim giving the students something to study in preparation for a test. Preaching is about bringing such energy and clarity and insight to the moment that the "students" don't need notes at all. The message is with them from that moment onward.

Question 9: Do on-screen visuals fit this approach?

On-screen visuals can be an important tool of communication, and I sometimes use them myself. In fact, I've often jokingly wondered, *What if Paul had had our common technology? Just think of the impact!* The use of on-screen visuals certainly can match an extemporaneous approach, though one can be tied to the main point(s) and quotes. The use of these tools is something of a blend, but it largely matches an extemporaneous approach. Of course no preacher should ever just read through his visuals and consider it a fine presentation.

As an aside, I've wondered if using on-screen visuals has left us too lazy to learn how to use the more powerful screen of the listener's imagination to bring the text and message alive. I avoided using visuals for so many years. At last I felt I could effectively create a message with enough interest and clarity that I was prepared to speak at a roadside, a campsite, a retreat center, or anywhere else where audiovisuals were unavailable and unusable.

Question 10: How does a preacher know when to stop preaching with notes and start preaching on his feet? Is this an issue of maturity?

Spurgeon observed that this comes with greater ease as a preacher ages because of his increased experience and knowledge. In this book I have explained how to transition and how to decide. In the final analysis the decision is what is at issue. The decision to learn to preach on your feet allows you to begin organizing the way you study and communicate and prepare so that you will learn a little and then a little more. Personally, it took me a period of about three years to learn how to preach on my feet and another two years to decide to make it my exclusive approach.

Question 11: How do you capture particularly apt phrasings or illustrations?

Most illustrations can be explained simply from memory without spending a lot of time studying them. I can thank Dennis Rainey of *FamilyLife Radio* for this insight. Some years ago I was promoting my book, *The Absolute Quickest Way to Help Your Child Change*, and was about to read an illustration from the book on air. Dennis looked at me and said, "Don't read it, just tell it." And of course I could tell it, and it was fresher and clearer than reading to an audience. Indeed, perhaps the radio is one of the proofs of the importance of being extemporaneous since simply getting on air and reading would create nothing but a dwindling audience. On the other hand, if there is an exact illustration or quote that demands exactitude when it's read, I carry the book with me (or the quote on a 3x5 card) and don't worry about it. Perhaps you should practice the exact phrasing until you are comfortable communicating it in day-to-day conversation.

Question 12: How prepared should the introduction or conclusion be?

The introduction and conclusion require no more (and no less) preparation than any other part of the sermon.

Question 13: How dependent is this approach on the speaker's personality type?

The preacher's personality can influence whether he is apt to preach on his feet. The definition of preaching in this book, in fact, must necessarily involve personality. My conviction is that there's no such thing as a personality that comes alive when you read a manuscript. All personalities can have a conversation, and in some ways preaching is simply having a conversation with a large group of people. Phillips Brooks seemed to think some people were made for this and others weren't, but Spurgeon's and Finney's arguments are compelling— that in the course of time anyone can learn to be a practiced thinker. Personality is entirely too individualized to make an absolute statement here. The fact remains, you'll never know until you try.

Question 14: Does this approach present special challenges to those preaching multiple services?

I preach three services every Sunday. What I have found is that each service has its own personality, so the message adapts slightly to each service. After I've preached, I normally apologize to the Lord for my failings (I learned this from Spurgeon). Next, I ask the Lord to emphasize the useful things I've said and erase the useless things I've said. Before I preach in the second service, I actually, and formally before the Lord, let go of the last message and pray as though I were about to deliver it for the first time. In my experience, if I try to get myself to remember to say something I said in the previous message, it invariably fouls up the next one. I often wish I had said some additional things to the audience, but back in my extensive-outline days I had the same regret.

Question 15: How fresh does an extemporaneous sermon need to be? How far in advance can such sermons be prepared?

In the final analysis a sermon must be at least refreshed; that is to say, spending at least a half an hour of reflection before giving a message with which you are intimately familiar is a valuable exercise in preparation. If you are really familiar with a message or a text, then the sermon can again burst into flames—much as true preachers experience in counseling or conversation or Bible study when they are going over familiar ground; it rekindles his heart and his memory because of his love for the Word and that truth for that moment in particular.

Question 16: How can you make sure you're correct about a particular point without either memorizing an explanation or exegetical point? Especially when there is a detail regarding language or the like?

You can be sure you're correct if you really learn the material. Often we look up information and collect a great amount of it but never genuinely learn it. Depth of learning is measured by "speed of access." In other words, if you can instantly, or almost instantly, recall something, you've learned it. For example, someone's name is learned when you can recall it whenever you need it. A phone number is learned when you can dial it when you need it. Is the information on a passage either so complicated that you can't learn it in time for the sermon or so new to you that you haven't yet truly learned it? If so, just avoid it. Preaching is not about your research but about your understanding. It is not about how much information you found but the clarity with which you communicate the information you know. Again, if you cannot retain the information (excepting an occasional lengthy quote, etc.), then neither will your listeners retain it unless they take copious notes which they must then study often in order to learn it. I remember learning an oversimplification of Wittgenstein's insight in college which stated, "If you can't say it, you don't know it." Imagine how diminished the enjoyment of a joke would be if someone simply found it one night and read it to you the next day. Not so good! If that's true with a mere joke, imagine how we diminish our understanding in preaching the Word of God by simply not learning the information.

Question 17: Without memorizing an outline, how do you come up with applications and illustrations on your feet?

As I have discussed at length in this book, preachers should reflect on applications and illustrations as part of the preparation process. You are not just hoping an illustration will arise; you prepare for them. But in the moment of delivery even better illustrations can appear—more pristine and more useful—than those anticipated or considered in the preparation phase of preaching on your feet. It is genuinely amazing how able the human mind is at filtering through material to come to the essence. Naturally, this skill takes time to develop, but you begin by filling your mind with as many illustrations and applications as you can. Having an abundant number in mind allows you to contrast them. Choosing the strategic few turns out to be a relatively obvious choice. Again, you experiment with this process to prove to yourself that it really matches our human design.

Question 18: What if you can't remember the whole message without a note or two? Wouldn't it be more honoring to God to have a note or two to remember what you have carefully studied and prepared to say?

Let's consider the second part of this question first, concerning "honoring God." Certainly standing before people and confusing them is not honoring to God. If those are your only choices—to use notes and communicate clearly or not use notes and communicate poorly—then of course use notes. The fact is, however, that this book demonstrates, supports, and hopes to convince the reader that notes are unnecessary and in most instances actually harmful to connecting the message in your heart to the need and understanding in your listener's heart.

Concerning the first part of the question, I don't believe anyone can remember a whole message without a significant amount of time simply memorizing a manuscript. Preaching on your feet is a genuine paradigm shift for most preachers because at its core it means that the preacher doesn't have to "remember the whole message." Instead, he understands the text and his point, and in the same way an animated conversation occurs. An animated message is born under the leading of the Spirit after thorough preparation.

Question 19: Don't some preachers preach more heart-to-heart with notes than many do without them? Are we attacking a problem the wrong way?

Some exceptional preachers are able to prepare a thick outline or a manuscript and bring it to life for an audience. Praise God for these individuals, and I would be the last person to suggest they abandon their ways. But most preachers do not have the necessary performance component in their personalities. The real question is, how can a preacher be better next Sunday than he was last Sunday? Comparing preachers is an unfair practice since God has given each a measure of faith. Not everyone can be Billy Graham, no matter their effort, with or without notes. The question is one each preacher must answer for himself. Would a preacher who preaches heart to heart with notes be more effective if he learned to preach heart to heart without them? Only trying "preaching on your feet" can answer that question.

Question 20: Can't this play into pride, such that an individual gains accolades as a starry-eyed parishioner exclaims, "My preacher doesn't even use notes—he's *so* godly!"

Pride seems to be an issue in every direction. It is just as easy to imagine parishioners exclaiming, as I've personally heard before, "My preacher studies 40 hours a week and fully prepares a manuscript and thorough notes for us." In any direction one goes, there can be the accusation or the reality of pride. At the heart of any conversation on preaching the Word of God is not the preacher but the listener. Is the listener's life changed by an encounter with the truth of God? Personally, my observation is that if it takes an individual 30 or 40 hours to prepare one message, then that person is in the wrong business. By this I mean that if 30 or 40 hours is necessary in order to preach one sermon, then we must ask, "Is this person truly competent with language, literature, and communication?" The answer may be, indeed, that this individual is simply not called to preach. But an equal possibility is that he is enslaved by his assumptions regarding manuscripts and notes. The principles in this book could indeed liberate him to be among the people during the week as part of his preparation for Sunday.

Question 21: How can I know that preaching on my feet will be more effective for me?

It is simply true that "we know what we know and we don't know what we don't know." No one can be confident he will be more effective in preaching on his feet until he actually preaches on his feet. It would be similar to asking, "How can I know that a freestyle stroke will be better than dog-paddling when I swim?" Could we agree that most swimmers swim better and faster in freestyle than dog-paddling? If so, then this book offers you that kind of convincing proof. On the other hand, no preacher can really know his effectiveness until he has personally mastered both approaches and can finally decide for himself before God.

Question 22: What do I do if I just can't seem to pull it off? Can I gradually shorten my notes and outlines?

This book outlines a process that takes you from where you are to using the principles of note-free preaching. Compared to reading a manuscript, using an outline with many sections of freedom is an excellent way to go, and a healthy transition. But Spurgeon once observed that a man who doesn't need a cane but uses one will come to need a cane. In other words, bringing notes into the pulpit can become a very addictive habit. A better way is excellent preparation, clear thinking, and a Spirit-led unfolding of the message.

Chapter 14

Could Preaching on Your Feet Change the World?

*I*t is rather simple logic.

Major premise: Preaching can change the world.

Minor premise: Preaching on your feet makes for better preaching.

Conclusion: Preaching on your feet can better change the world.

Naturally, some might not agree that extemporaneous preaching is more effective than preaching from a manuscript or thick notes. However, subjectively speaking, only the person who can preach both with manuscripts and extemporaneously is qualified to have a legitimate opinion. I say "subjectively" because the effectiveness of a speaker is not given entirely to scientific inquiry. Popularity is one thing and impact is another, though it is worth noting that it is hard to imagine an unpopular or unnoticed speaker who preaches with high impact. Finney made a tremendous if not glorious claim when he said:

> We shall never have a set of men in our halls of legislation, in our courts of justice, and in our pulpits, who are powerful and overwhelming speakers, and can carry the world before them, till our system of education teaches them to think, closely, rapidly, consecutively, and till all their habits of speaking in the schools are extemporaneous. The very style of communicating thought, in what is commonly called a good style of writing, is not calculated to leave a deep impression. It is not laconic, direct, pertinent. It is not the language of nature.[1]

There are two noteworthy things in Finney's quote. One is about impact, and the other is about education. Impact, in Finney's thinking, was beyond that of the pulpit and the church. He saw this approach to communication as effective no matter its venue. It certainly stands to reason that the church can have an impact beyond its walls as it prepares and affects members of society for every corner and crevice of useful contribution. In parallel, one might think of the popular singers and musicians over the decades. How many have gotten their start in a church choir, performing before a church audience? The exact number is likely immeasurable. What if churches regained prominence as true, effective training stations for leaders in the halls of education and

---

[1] Charles G. Finney, *Lectures on Revivals of Religion* (New York: Revell, 1868), 207–8.

justice, and in the pulpits throughout the world? The impact would be immeasurable and inspiring.

Finney's second point concerns education and specifically argues that training in his day was not teaching individuals to "think, closely, rapidly, consecutively, and till all their habits of speaking in the schools [were] extemporaneous." These are surprising words, coming from a man who went on to become president of Oberlin College. Today few schools teach their students to think on their feet; the exceptions are mostly law school and a few other exceptional schools like St. John's College in Annapolis, Maryland, and Santa Fe, New Mexico. Most of us who have learned to speak on our feet are self-taught.

The self-taught Spurgeon described these skills as belonging to "a practiced thinker—a man of information, meditating on his legs, and allowing his thoughts to march through his mouth into the open air. Think aloud as much as you can when you're alone, and you will soon be on the high road of success in this matter."[2] Spurgeon's advice is perhaps the most powerful in being self-taught, that is, learning to think aloud as much as you can when you're alone. It is even more powerful to think aloud with others who are gracious and keen in spirited interaction on valuable subjects.

Why Preaching on Your Feet
Can Change the World

The impact of Christianity through the centuries has been directly related to the public proclamation of God's Word. Even though there have also been revivals born through

---

[2] C. H. Spurgeon, *Lectures to My Students* (Grand Rapids: Zondervan, 1954), 149.

prayer and other methodologies, the truth must, in the final analysis, be proclaimed. The Bible itself shows this history of a neglect of the Word of God and a rebirth of its proclamation as found in examples such as Ezra, and clearly in the advent of Christ's public ministry. Our world, however, is a very diverse place and involves divergent worldviews, orientations, and economies such that we speak in terms of the Western world, the Eastern world, and the Third World. I believe a better way to think about the various situations in which preaching on your feet can make the difference is found in both literate and illiterate contexts.

Preaching on your feet is uniquely adaptable to both literate and illiterate contexts, but a literate audience is always the most challenging. An educated audience is one in which the members have both a Bible and note-taking equipment in hand, the Bible is referenced frequently, and copious notes may be penned for future reflection. Nothing inherent in preaching on your feet means such note taking and deep exposition must be avoided. Note taking, however, is not a necessity with preaching on your feet as it normally is with manuscripts and thick outlines. When a preacher uses ink and paper copiously and meticulously to organize information, then the level of complexity will demand that those who listen, if they hope to grasp the information and use it, must have a complete set of notes before them. This perfectly explains why many preachers hand out notes or outlines for the sermon. No doubt, this is an effective approach if the goal is to give the audience a complete set of notes (if not, they'll ask for them!). Preaching on your feet, however, has at its core the genuine probability that note taking will be unnecessary because the organization of material as it matches the passage will be memorable. Simply put, one who masters preaching on your feet is the one who must organize the material simply enough to be remembered easily for himself; and of course, if it is easy to remember for himself, it will most likely be easy to remember for the audience.

And what of the illiterate world? I've spent a fair amount of time in the rural sections of Uganda, where most of the people are illiterate though great efforts are being made to create a literate population—schools with all the children at play in matching uniforms abound throughout the countryside. Being able to read and write is supreme in this blossoming democracy. Imagine, however, a preacher with a full set of notes laying out point after point after point to a population of those who live off the land and who are hoping for better things for their own children. They can't afford paper and pen, and they can hardly retain the complexity that normally attends a manuscripted sermon. It is perfectly understandable how Third World preachers preach—with emotion, energy, fire, and stories—but often without much to say about the text itself. Preaching on your feet—and I hesitate to say these words—is the answer for preachers in these regions. Preaching on your feet is a habit and a skill. That is, if a practiced thinker has deeply interacted with the text but has also simplified the way he thinks about the information in order to share it clearly and cleanly from his heart to his illiterate but teachable congregation, how indeed might this change the world?

Why Preaching on Your Feet
Could Change the World

After many years in ministry, I have concluded that it is difficult to think straight and walk crooked. Preaching on your feet is about thinking straight and helping the listener think straight as well. Much of our preaching is either so complex, or so simple and low shelf, that neither really impacts the thinking process of the listener. Preaching on your feet requires a balanced approach. It requires the preacher to understand the text in such a way that he can stand on his feet and speak straight to the audience. Standing on your feet and speaking straight to an audience also means the audience can understand your message, remember it, reflect on it, and share it with others. It is difficult to imagine how such an approach, if indeed it allows the Word to reach into the depths of listeners, could not but change the world. And yet, even as we talk about changing the world in an all but clichéd way, perhaps we must remember that the impact is beyond this world.

Advantages of Preaching on Your Feet

Let us recap seven advantages of preaching on your feet. These advantages are essential to the way this approach can impact the world.

1. Study

Those who learn the skills involved in preaching on your feet simply have more time and opportunity to study and reflect on the Word of God and the insights of other thinkers. It is simple enough to understand why one who manuscripts or works on a thick outline must spend a great deal of time in that practice; perhaps that practice helps drive the message into one's soul, but it is incredibly time-consuming to write out large amounts of material. Not everyone has the personality design to do that much writing, but everyone has a personality which can reflect, which biblically is called meditation. There is also a different kind of rigor in profound reflection. Almost everyone who has ever spent any time in school knows how many notes they have taken and how little they have retained. The reason is rather simple; for the most part, when one is taking notes, he is not thinking.

2. Readiness

Preaching on your feet develops readiness for any speaking situation. Rather than trying to schedule enough time to prepare for a talk at a civic club or a Christian school or a Bible study, one who has learned the fine art of preaching on your feet can provide time for reflection on passages of deep familiarity and is ready "at a moment's notice" to speak well before an audience. Naturally, this readiness improves with practice and age.

3. Time

Time is among the great advantages of preaching on your feet. It is not simply that one has more time for study but that one optimizes his time because everything involved in ministry can be integrated immediately, and sometimes surprisingly, into the next message. Only a generation ago, the old preachers will tell you, they preached a number of times every week. Today most preachers speak only once. Surely, in part, this has been caused by abandoning the age-old practice of extemporaneous preaching. Time can be available for family, for service to others, for rest, or for more ministry opportunities. Preaching on your feet returns time to the preacher because of its efficiency. How one invests his time is another matter entirely.

4. Uniqueness

Preaching on your feet unleashes the uniqueness of the individual. Only the best of actors can take a manuscript and refreshingly communicate their unique personality, while most others cannot. Preaching on your feet engages the personality of the preacher because he must be engaged in order to communicate what he has reflected upon carefully. Preaching is the communication of truth through the personality as the Spirit leads. Therefore, it stands to reason that this engaged, direct, heart-to-heart approach allows for the individual's voice by God's design to bring forth truth in a never-before-heard way for that moment in time.

5. Connection

Preaching on your feet has the advantage of connection. Spurgeon compared this with pleading before a judge for a friend. This kind of pleading happens in the moment and is extemporaneous and "on your feet." Since there is no obligation to follow a manuscript, you can always adapt to the circumstances of the moment. When an audience is not engaged, you can adjust; add a story, a look, an honest thought; and reengage the congregation. Preaching on your feet encourages you to connect directly with your audience in the easiest and most effective of ways.

6. Spirit Dependence

Preaching on your feet provides for a greater and more immediate dependence on the Spirit. Certainly any diligent and faithful servant can be Spirit led whether he is working on a manuscript or sharing it before an audience. The advantage of preaching on your feet, however, is that it demands a greater dependence at the point of delivery.

The preacher who uses a manuscript may have a noble attitude, but the truth remains that he is relying on the manuscript and hopeful that the Lord will use it. No doubt that the Lord will use it, but how easily could he turn from a point at the Spirit's direction during a message? The danger spontaneity brings is its greatest advantage because it allows the individual to turn on a dime if the Spirit of God says, "Turn!"

7. God's Glory

All preaching can certainly glorify God, but preaching on your feet has the upper hand on bringing God glory. It is difficult to explain how shocking, awesome, and overwhelming the kindness of God seems to the preacher who has studied hard and labored in prayer, to then speak before the people, seeing unique insights arise in the moment of preaching—such that he too is surprised and grateful for this kindness of God. This individual knows how magnificently God appeared in the moment. This is not to say that the use of manuscripts and thick outlines can't have God's glory imbued with hope. Nevertheless, there is still the temptation that the skills, the talents, the hard work, and the editing are magnified in such a way so as to dim, if only slightly, the glory of God.

Conclusion

When I graduated from doctoral studies at Phoenix Seminary, I listened with joyful attention as different speakers congratulated us on the conclusion of our hard work and the anticipation of our great hopes. Curiously, God provided three speakers which perfectly illustrate the point. One graduating student represented the class and read a nice speech which I greatly appreciated for her time and efforts. The primary speaker, who gave the charge to the graduating class was energetic and alive, but used notes and gave us 10 major points to remember as we were sent out to minister. With some effort I can recollect three of those points, and all of us were hoping to get an audio copy or a printed set of notes in order to review it again. A third speaker only spoke briefly. He was from a racial minority. He had no notes though he had clearly thought about what he wanted to say. I remember his message. He spoke from his heart of his gratitude for the opportunity to have studied at such an institution. He spoke from his heart about the Word touching others in his community. When he was through, we didn't want his set of notes; we simply wanted to be like him.

Bibliography

Barth, Karl. *The Preaching of the Gospel*, trans. B. E. Hooke. Philadelphia: Westminster, 1963.

Broadus, John A. *On the Preparation and Delivery of Sermons*, 4th ed., rev. Vernon L. Stanfield. San Francisco: Harper & Row, 1979. Originally published 1879.

Brooks, Phillips. *The Joy of Preaching*, with a foreword by Warren W. Wiersbe. Grand Rapids: Kregel Publications, 1989. Originally published as *Lectures on Preaching*, 1877.

Buckley, James M., LL.D. *Extemporaneous Oratory for Professional and Amateur Speakers*. New York: Eaton & Mains, 1898.

Dallimore, Arnold A. *George Whitefield: God's Anointed Servant in the Great Revival of the Eighteenth Century*. Wheaton, IL: Crossway, 1990.

————. *Spurgeon*. Chicago: Moody, 1984.

Finney, Charles G. *Charles G. Finney: An Autobiography*. Westwood, NJ: Fleming H. Revell, 1876.

Gibbs, Alfred P. *The Preacher and His Preaching*, 6th ed. Kansas City, KS: Walterick Publishers, n.d.

Howard, Ken. *Act Natural: How to Speak to Any Audience.* New York: Random House, 2003.

Koller, Charles W. *How to Preach without Notes.* Grand Rapids: Baker, 1964.

Larsen, David L. *The Company of the Preachers: A History of Biblical Preaching from the Old Testament to the Modern Era.* Grand Rapids: Kregel, 1998.

Lewis, Ralph L. *Persuasive Preaching Today.* Ann Arbor, MI: LithoCrafters, 1979.

Macartney, Clarence Edward. *Preaching without Notes.* Grand Rapids: Baker, 1946.

McDill, Wayne V. *The Moment of Truth: A Guide to Effective Sermon Delivery.* Nashville: Broadman & Holman, 1999.

Reid, Clyde. *The Empty Pulpit.* New York: Harper & Row, 1967.

Richard, Ramesh. *Preparing Expository Sermons: A Seven-Step Method for Biblical Preaching.* Grand Rapids: Baker, 1995.

Robinson, Haddon W. *Biblical Preaching.* Grand Rapids: Baker, 1980.

Spurgeon, Charles Haddon. "How Saints May Help the Devil," *Spurgeon's Sermons,* vol. 6. Grand Rapids: Baker, n.d. reprint; New York: Robert Carter & Brothers, 1883.

_____. *Lectures to My Students, Complete and Unabridged,* new ed. Containing selected lectures from series 1, 2, and 3. Grand Rapids: Zondervan, Ministry Resources Library, 1954.

_____. *The Soul-Winner: How to Lead Sinners to the Savior*. Grand Rapids: Wm. B. Eerdmans, 1963.

Stanley, Andy, and Jones, Lane. *Communicating for a Change: Seven Keys to Irresistible Communication*. Sisters, OR: Multnomah, 2006.

Unger, Merrill F. *Principles of Expository Preaching*. Grand Rapids: Zondervan, 1955.

Ware, Henry, Jr. *Hints on Extemporaneous Preaching*. [book on-line] Boston: Hilliard, Gray, Little, and Wilkins, (James Loring, printer, 1831), accessed 11 January 2006; available from http://www.americanunitarian.org/warextemp.htm; Internet.

Webb, Joseph M. *Preaching without Notes*. Nashville: Abingdon, 2001.

Wenger, Win, and Richard Poe. *The Einstein Factor: A Proven New Method for Increasing Your Intelligence*. Rocklin, CA: Prima Publishing, 1996.

Williams, Roy H. "Blogs and Reality TV: The Changing Face of America," (article on-line) *Monday Morning Memo*, Wizard Academy, 20 February 2006 available from http://www.wizardacademy.com/showmemo.asp?id=289; Internet; accessed 20 February 2006.

Additional Sources

Blackwood, Andrew W. *Preaching from the Bible*. Nashville: Abingdon, 1941.

Clinton, J. Robert. *The Making of a Leader*. Colorado Springs, CO: NavPress, 1988.

McDill, Wayne. *12 Essential Skills for Great Preaching*, 2nd ed., rev. Nashville: Broadman & Holman, 2006.

McLuhan and Davies Communications, Inc. / Think on Your Feet International, Inc. Ph: (403) 277-9230 Toll Free: 1-800-453-1611, or *www.thinkonyourfeet.com*. After completing the manuscript for *Preach on Your Feet*, I was introduced to the excellent training offered by McLuhan and Davies. The material is primarily for communication in general, but the training is certainly helpful to preachers and communicators of all types. And yes, the title was adapted from the idiom and their course name.

Worley, Robert C. *Preaching and Teaching in the Earliest Church*. Philadelphia: Westminster, 1967.

Name Index

Subject Index

Scripture Index